T0065391

THE RULE OF SAINT AUGUSTINE

THE RULE OF
SAINT AUGUSTINE

with Introduction and Commentary by
TARSICIUS J. VAN BAVEL osa

Translated by
RAYMOND CANNING osa

IMAGE BOOKS
A Division of Doubleday & Company, Inc.
Garden City, New York
1986

Library of Congress Cataloging-in-Publication Data

Augustine, Saint, Bishop of Hippo.
The rule of Saint Augustine.

Translation of: Regula.
1. Augustinians—Rules. I. Bavel, Tarsicius
J. van. II. Title.
BX2904.E5 1986   255'.406   85-20760
ISBN 0-385-23241-1

ISBN 978-0-385-23241-8

CONTENTS

INTRODUCTION TO THE RULE

INTRODUCTION TO THE RULE
of Augustine of Hippo (354–430)

Text

Augustine is well known as the restless searcher for truth,
as the convert, bishop and scholar. He is less well known
as a monk. We can only fully understand his personality,
however, if we keep in mind that his sole wish after his
conversion was to be 'a servant of God'; that is, a monk.
He lived also as a monk when he was a priest, and even
later as bishop. But there is more to it than that. In writing
the oldest monastic Rule in the West, Augustine exerted
an unusually great influence on the Christian ideal of the
religious life. In this way his role in the development of
Western monasticism has been highly significant.

In the course of the centuries a number of different
monastic Rules have borne the name of Augustine: a 'Rule
for women' (*Regularis informatio*), a 'Rule for men' (*Prae-
ceptum*) and a 'Regulation for a monastery' (*Ordo monas-
terii*). These have come down to us in no fewer than nine
different forms. The most recent research, however, has
shown that only one of them is attributable to Augustine
himself. Pioneering work in this field has been done
especially by Dr L. Verheijen osa. After years of research
he has offered us a critical Latin text of the Rule of Augustine in his monumental two-volume work, *La Règle de
Saint Augustin* (Paris 1967). We have based our English

translation (in both the feminine and the masculine form) on this text.

Historical background

Augustine wrote his Rule around the year 397, about ten years after he had been baptized by Ambrose in Milan. By 397 Augustine had already been through a certain period of experience of the religious life, for his first foundation had taken place in 388 at Tagaste. Later, as a priest, he founded a monastery for lay-brothers in Hippo (391). And, when he became a bishop, he set up a monastery for clerics in his bishop's house in Hippo (395/6). It was there that, around 397, Augustine wrote his Rule. From a historical perspective, then, the Rule of Augustine stems from the early period of religious life. The Egyptian desert can be considered the cradle of the movement which later came to be referred to in general as 'the religious life'. The oldest regulations for communities of monks were composed by Pachomius (*c.* 292–346/7) in Tabennêsi (in the southern part of Upper Egypt). His successor, Horsiesius (*c.* 300–*c.* 388), also left behind an important monastic testament, namely 'The Book of our Father Horsiesius'. And later we have the 'Great and Small Rules' of Basil, the bishop of Caesarea (*c.* 330–379). It was probably around 370 that the monastic form of life began to appear also in the West, only thirty years before the first extant Western monastic Rule, that of Augustine, was written. A good hundred years later Benedict of Nursia (*c.* 480–*c.* 547) was to write his well-known Rule, drawing upon both the Eastern and Western traditions.

Influence

The influence of the Rule of Augustine is apparent from the fact that fourteen manuscripts from before the year

1000 have been preserved; the oldest of these dates from the sixth century. This influence can also be ascertained from the use made of the Rule of Augustine by writers in Gaul, Spain and Italy during the two centuries following Augustine's death. In compiling norms for male and female religious in their milieu they quote certain sections from the Rule of Augustine. The best known of these writers are: Fulgentius of Ruspe (462/8–527/33); Caesarius of Arles (c. 470–542); Leander of Seville (c. 545–600/1); Isidore of Seville (c. 560–636), the author of 'The Rule of the Master'; and Benedict of Nursia.

Thus it can be seen that the Rule of Augustine was copied in many different regions, and in this way it came to be widely distributed. This proves that there were people who lived from the inspiration that the Rule offered. But we should not look at this too one-sidedly. Before the year 1000 the Rule of Augustine was always handed on together with other Rules and monastic documents. Thus, different religious currents flowed into the one great tradition. This 'tradition of the Fathers' as a whole was offered to the religious of that time as a source of inspiration. Only between the ninth and the eleventh centuries does the Rule of Augustine appear as a rule of life valid in itself for a definite group of religious. These centuries are precisely the period during which a reform of monastic life and of the diocesan clergy was carried through. In this reform the Rule of Augustine played an important role and it was accepted by different groups as their only rule of life.

Observance over the centuries

From the eleventh century on, the Rule of Augustine spread like fire among stubble. It would be impossible to give a description of its diffusion from the early Middle Ages up to the present day. We can only attempt to list some of the groups which have adopted the Rule. Among the foundations of male religious there are: the Canons Regular of Saint Augustine; the Canons Regular of Prémontré (Norbertines); the Croisiers; several orders of Knights; the Trinitarians; the Mercedarians; the Dominicans; the Augustinian Hermits or Friars; the Augustinian Recollects; the Servites; the Alexians; the John of God Brothers and those of Trier; the Piarists; and the Assumptionists. Numerous women's foundations also patterned their lives on the Rule of Augustine: the Brigittines; the Annunciates of Lombardy; the Canonesses of the Holy Sepulchre; the Augustinian Sisters of Meaux; the Ursulines; the Canonesses of Saint Augustine; the Visitation Order of Francis de Sales; the Order of our Lady of Refuge and the Sisters of the Good Shepherd founded by Jean Eudes; Les Dames de St Thomas de Villeneuve; the Sisters of St Monica; the Sisters of St Rita. In particular, many congregations which devote themselves to nursing and the care of the sick, such as the Black Sisters and the Hospital Sisters, have chosen the Rule of Augustine as the source of inspiration for their communities. This list is incomplete. In all, several hundred Orders and Congregations – some of which have now ceased to exist – have adopted the Rule of Augustine.

Character of the Rule

1   The Rule clearly gives the impression of being a summary of oral conferences which Augustine held for his monks. The ideas are not teased out; they are simply rendered in a very concise manner. They were presumed to be well known already, and a certain familiarity with Augustine's other works is necessary in order to penetrate to the deeper meaning of the Rule's short sentences. Parallel texts from other works can clarify the Rule and

give insight into it. For Augustine's followers the Rule was certainly a summary designed to refresh the memory.

2   The Rule of Augustine covers only a few pages, and its principal purpose is to offer some important thoughts which can provide inspiration. These thoughts are based particularly on the Scriptures. In the short text of the Rule there are at least thirty-five references to the Scriptures: eight to the Old Testament and twenty-seven to the New. Even the simplest sentences are interlaced with biblical ideas which provide the basic inspiration. In these references to the Scriptures Augustine's own vision and spirituality come to light, for the biblical ideas which he emphasizes are the cherished sources from which he himself lives. It is precisely this biblical and evangelic foundation which forms the permanent structure of the Rule: it guarantees the Rule's value throughout changing times and cultures.

3   The fundamental ideas of the Rule are built up around the ideal of the Jerusalem community from Acts 4:31–5. Love and community here have pride of place: a good community life is nothing other than the practice of love. It is immediately obvious how few concrete regulations and detailed laws are given in the Rule. Nowhere is it a question of details, but of the core of things and the human heart. Thus, the way of interiorization is repeatedly applied in the Rule: the external alone is not sufficient, for it must be the symbol of what happens inwardly. The external ought not to remain empty, but should be animated from within. The final characteristic in this regard is the almost total absence of emphasis on 'asceticism'; that is, leading an ascetical life in a material sense by denying oneself food and drink, or by self-chastisement. The accent shifts more to life in community as a victory over self-seeking. What the Rule asks is that attention should be directed to the upbuilding of relationships of love.

4   Pachomius, Basil and Augustine all laid great stress on community life. The reason for this was that they were convinced that the orientation to one's own self and individualism formed the greatest obstacle to the realization of the gospel. For them the first community of Jerusalem plays the role of an ancient dream which becomes an ideal for the present and for the future. We could characterize the Rule of Augustine as a call to the evangelical equality of all people. It voices the Christian demand to bring all men and women into full community. At the same time it sounds an implicit protest against inequality in a society which is so clearly marked by possessiveness, pride and power. According to Augustine, therefore, a monastic community should offer an alternative by striving to build up a community that is not motivated by possessiveness, pride and power, but by love for one another. And, in this sense, the Rule of Augustine is also socially critical.

THE RULE OF AUGUSTINE

This translation is based on the Latin text in the critical edition provided by L. Verheijen OSA, *La Règle de Saint Augustin. I: Tradition Manuscrite*, Paris, 1967, p. 417–37. It is an interpretative translation, intended for the everyday use of modern readers. In this it follows closely the Dutch version produced by Tarsicius J. van Bavel, *Augustinus van Hippo. Regel voor de Gemeenschap*, Averbode, 1982. Specialist readers are referred to the critical articles of L. Verheijen, published in his book: *Nouvelle approche de la Règle de Saint Augustin*, Bégrolles-en-Mauges, Abbaye de Bellefontaine, 1980.

The Rule of Augustine
(*Masculine Version*)

1 THE BASIC IDEAL: MUTUAL LOVE EXPRESSED IN THE COMMUNITY OF GOODS AND IN HUMILITY

1. We urge you who form a religious community to put the following precepts into practice.

2. Before all else, *live together in harmony* (Ps. 67 (68):7), *being of one mind and one heart* (Acts 4:32) on the way to God. For is it not precisely for this reason that you have come to live together?

3. Among you there can be no question of personal property. Rather, take care that you share everything in common. Your superior should see to it that each person is provided with food and clothing. He does not have to give exactly the same to everyone, for you are not all equally strong, but each person should be given what he personally needs. For this is what you read in the Acts of the Apostles: '*Everything they owned was held in common, and each one received whatever he had need of*' (Acts 4:32; 4:35).

4. Those who owned possessions in the world should readily agree that, from the moment they enter the religious life, these things become the property of the community.

5. But those who did not have possessions ought not to strive in the religious community for what they could not obtain outside it. One must indeed have regard for their frailty by providing them with whatever they need, even if they were formerly so poor that they could not even afford the very necessities of life. They may not, however, consider themselves fortunate because they now receive food and clothing which were beyond their means in their earlier lives.

6. Nor should they give themselves airs because they now find themselves in the company of people whom they would not have ventured to approach before. Their hearts should seek the nobler things, not vain earthly appearances. If, in the religious life, rich people were to become humble and poor people haughty, then this style of life would seem to be of value only to the rich and not to the poor.

7. On the other hand, let those who appear to have had some standing in the world not look down upon their brothers who have entered the religious community from a condition of poverty. They ought to be more mindful of their life together with poor brothers than of the social status of their wealthy parents. And the fact that they have made some of their possessions available to the community gives them no reason to have a high opinion of themselves. Otherwise people would more easily fall prey to pride in sharing their riches with the community than they would have done if they had enjoyed them in the world. For while all vices manifest themselves in wrongdoing, pride lurks also in our good works, seeking to destroy even them. What good does it do to distribute one's possessions to the poor and to become poor oneself, if giving up riches makes a person prouder than he was when he had a fortune?

8. You are all to live together, therefore, *one in mind and one in heart* (cf. Acts 4:32), and honour God in one another, because *each of you has become his temple* (2 Cor. 6:16).

2 COMMUNITY PRAYER

1. *Persevere faithfully in prayer* (Col. 4:2) at the hours and times appointed.

2. The place of prayer should not be used for any purpose other than that for which it is intended and from which it takes its name. Thus if someone wants to pray there even outside the appointed hours, in his own free time, he should be able to do so without being hindered by others who have no business being there.

3. When you pray to God in psalms and songs, the words spoken by your lips should also be alive in your hearts.

4. When you sing, keep to the text you have, and do not sing what is not intended to be sung.

3 COMMUNITY AND CARE OF THE BODY

1. As far as your health allows, keep your bodily appetites in check by fasting and abstinence from food and

drink. Those who are unable to fast the whole day may have something to eat before the main meal which takes place in the late afternoon. They may do this, however, only around midday. But the sick may have something to eat at any time of the day.

2. From the beginning of the meal to the end listen to the customary reading without noise or protest against the Scriptures, for you have not only to satisfy your physical hunger, *but also to hunger for the word of God* (cf. Amos 8:11).

3. There are some who are weaker because of their former manner of life. If an exception is made for them at table, those who are stronger because they have come from a different way of life ought not to take this amiss or to consider it unfair. They should not think that the others are more fortunate because they receive better food. Let them rather be glad that they are capable of something which is beyond the strength of the others.

4. There-are some who, before entering the religious life, were accustomed to living comfortably, and therefore they receive something more in the way of food and clothing: better bedding, perhaps, or more blankets. The others who are stronger, and therefore happier, do not receive these things. But, taking into account the former habits of life of the rich, keep in mind how much they now have to do without, even though they cannot live as simply as those who are physically stronger. Not everyone should want to have the extra he sees another receive, for this is done not to show favour but only out of concern for the person. Otherwise a deplorable disorder would creep into the religious life, whereby the poor begin to drift

easily along while the rich put themselves out in every possible way.

5. The sick should obviously receive suitable food; otherwise their illness would only get worse. Once they are over the worst of their sickness, they ought to be well cared for so that they may be fully restored to health as quickly as possible. And this holds good even if they formerly belonged to the very poorest class in society. During their convalescence they should receive the same that the rich are entitled to because of their former manner of life. But once they have made a complete recovery they are to go back to living as they did earlier on, when they were happier because their needs were fewer. The simpler a way of life, the better it is suited to servants of God.

When a sick person has been restored to health, he will have to be careful not to become the slave of his own desires. He will have to part with the privileges granted because of his illness. Those who have the strength to lead simple lives should consider themselves the richest of people. For it is better to be able to make do with a little than to have plenty.

4 MUTUAL RESPONSIBILITY IN GOOD AND EVIL

1. Do not attract attention by the way you dress. Endeavour to impress by your manner of life, not by the clothes you wear.

2. When you go out, go with somebody else, and stay together when you have reached your destination.

3. Whatever you are doing, your behaviour should in no way cause offence to anyone, but should rather be in keeping with the holiness of your way of life.

4. When you see a woman, do not keep provocatively looking at her. Of course, no one can forbid you to see women when you go out, *but it is wrong to desire a woman or to want her to desire you* (cf. Matt. 5:28). For it is not only by affectionate embraces that desire between man and woman is awakened, but also by looks. You cannot say that your inner attitude is good if with your eyes you desire to possess a woman, for the eye is the herald of the heart. And if people allow their impure intentions to appear, albeit without words but just by looking at each other and finding pleasure in each other's passion, even though not in each other's arms, we cannot speak any longer of true chastity which is precisely that of the heart.

5. Indeed, if a person cannot keep his eyes off a woman and enjoys attracting her attention, he should not imagine that others do not see this. Of course they see it; even people you would not expect notice it. But even if it did remain concealed and unseen by men, will it not be seen by *God who scans the heart of every man* (Prov. 24:12) and from whom nothing is hidden? Or are we to imagine that *God does not see it* (Ps. 93(94):7), because just as his wisdom is far beyond ours, so too is he prepared to be extraordinarily patient with us? A religious should be afraid *to offend the God of love* (Prov. 24:18); for the sake of this love he ought to be ready to give up a sinful love for a woman. Whoever is mindful that God sees all things will not wish to look at a woman with sinful desire. For, precisely on this point, the text of Scripture, *'the Lord abhors a covetous eye'* (Prov. 27:20: LXX), impresses upon us that we are to stand in awe of him.

6. Therefore, in church or wherever you may be in the
    company of women, you are to consider yourselves
    responsible for one another's chastity. Then *God who
    dwells in you* (2 Cor. 6:16) will watch over you
    through your responsibility for one another.

7. If you notice in a brother this provocative look I
    have spoken of, then warn him immediately, so that
    the evil that has taken root may not worsen and so
    that he may promptly improve his behaviour.

8. If after this admonition you see him doing the same
    thing again, anyone who notices it should consider
    him a sick person in need of treatment. At that time
    no one is any longer free to be silent. *First inform one
    or two others of the situation so that with two or three you
    may be able to convince* him of his fault (Matt.
    18:15–17) and to call him to order with due firmness. Do not
    think that you are acting out of ill-will in doing this.
    On the contrary, you would be at fault if by your
    silence you allow your brothers to meet their down-
    fall, when by speaking you could set them on the
    right path.

    Imagine, for example, that your brother had a
    physical wound which he wanted to conceal for fear
    of undergoing medical treatment. Would it not be
    heartless of us to say nothing about it? Rather, would
    it not be an act of mercy on our part to make it
    known? How much greater, then, is our obligation
    to make our brother's condition known and to
    prevent evil gaining a stronger hold in his heart,
    something much worse than a physical wound.

9. If he does not wish to listen to your warning, then
    first advise the superior so that he and the brother
    may talk the matter out in private, and in this way
    others will not need to know of it or be involved. If

he is still unwilling to listen, then you may bring in others to convince him of his fault. If he still persists in denying it, then, without his knowledge, others must be brought in, so that *his faults may be pointed out* to him *by more than a single witness in the presence of all* (1 Tim. 5:20), for the word of two or three witnesses is more convincing than that of one.

Once his guilt has been established, it is up to the superior or even to the priest under whose jurisdiction the religious house falls, to determine which punishment he should best undergo with a view to his improvement. If he refuses to submit to this punishment, he is to be sent away from the community, even though he himself may be unwilling to go. Here again this action is not prompted by heartlessness but by love, for in this way he is prevented from having a bad influence on others and contributing to their downfall too.

10.   What I have said about looking at a woman lustfully holds too for other sins. In discovering, warding off, bringing to light, proving and punishing all other faults, you are faithfully and diligently to follow the procedure set out above, always with love for the people involved but with aversion for their faults.

11.   If a brother of his own accord confesses that he has gone so far along the wrong path as to receive letters and gifts secretly from a woman, we ought to deal with him gently and to pray for him. But if he is found out and proved guilty, he is to be severely punished according to the judgement of the priest or the superior.

5 SERVICE OF ONE ANOTHER

1. Your clothes should be looked after in common by one or more brothers who are to see that they are well aired and kept free from moths. Just as the food you eat is prepared in the one kitchen, so the clothes you wear are to come from the one storeroom.

   And, as far as possible, it should not matter to you greatly which summer or winter clothes you receive. It does not make any difference whether you get back the same clothes you handed in or something that has been worn by another, *provided no one is denied what he needs* (Acts 4:35). If this gives rise to jealousy or grumbling, or if people begin complaining that the clothes they now have are not as good as those they had before, or if they think it beneath them to wear clothes that have previously been worn by others, does that not tell you something? If the external matter of dress becomes a cause of discord, does this not prove that inwardly, in the attitude of your heart, there is something sadly lacking? But if you are unable to do these things and your weakness is taken into consideration so that you are allowed to receive again the same clothes you handed in, even so, keep them all in the one place where they will be looked after by those charged with this task.

2. The intention behind all this is that no one will seek his own advantage in his work. Everything you do is to be for the service of the community, and you are to work with more zeal and more enthusiasm than if each person were merely working for himself and his own interests. For it is written of love that '*it is not self-seeking*' (1 Cor. 13:5); that is to say, love puts the interests of the community before personal advantage,

and not the other way around. Therefore the degree
to which you are concerned for the interests of the
community rather than for your own, is the criterion
by which you can judge how much progress you have
made. Thus in all the fleeting necessities of human life
something sublime and permanent reveals itself, *namely
love* (cf. 1 Cor. 12:31; 13:13).

3. It follows from this that a religious who receives
clothes or other useful items from his parents or relatives may not keep these quietly for himself. He
should place them at the disposal of the superior. *Once
they have become the property of the community, it is up
to the superior to see that these articles find their way into
the hands of those who need them* (Acts 4:32; 4:35).

4. When you want to wash your clothes or have them
washed at a laundry, let this take place in consultation
with the superior lest an exaggerated desire for clean
clothes sully your character.

5. Because bathing may be necessary for good health,
the opportunity to visit the public baths may never be
refused. In this matter follow medical advice without
grumbling. Even if a person is unwilling, he shall do
what has to be done for the good of his health, if
necessary at the command of the superior. But if
someone wants to go bathing just because he enjoys
it, when it is not really necessary, he will have to
learn to renounce his desires. For what a person likes
may not always be good for him. It may even be
harmful.

6. In any case, if a brother says that he does not feel
well, even though he is not noticeably sick, believe
him without hesitation. But if you are not sure
whether the treatment he wishes to have will be of
any benefit to him, then consult a doctor about it.

7. See to it that there are always two or more of you
    when you visit the public baths. Indeed, this applies
    wherever you go. And it is not for you to choose the
    people who will go with you; you are to leave this to
    the decision of the superior.

8. Someone should be deputed by the community to
    care for the sick. At the same time this person ought
    to take care of those who are convalescing and those
    who are weak even though they are not running a
    temperature. The infirmarian may take from the
    kitchen whatever he himself considers necessary.

9. Those responsible for food, clothes and books
    should serve their brothers without grumbling.

10. Books will be available every day at the appointed
    hour, and not at any other time.

11. The brothers in charge of clothes and shoes should
    not delay in making these available to those who need
    them.

6 LOVE AND CONFLICT

1. Do not quarrel. But if you do have a quarrel, put
    an end to it as quickly as possible. Otherwise an
    isolated moment of anger grows into hatred, *the
    splinter becomes a beam* (Matt. 7:3–5), and you make
    your heart a murderer's den. For we read in the Scrip-
    tures: *'Whoever hates his brother is a murderer'* (1 John
    3:15).

2. If you have hurt a person by abusing him, or by cursing or grossly accusing him, be careful to make amends for the harm you have done, as quickly as possible, by apologizing to him. And the one who has been hurt should be ready in his turn to forgive you without wrangling. Brothers who have insulted each other should *forgive each other's trespasses* (Matt. 6:12); if you fail to do this, your praying the Our Father becomes a lie. Indeed, the more you pray, the more honest your prayer ought to become.

It is better to have to deal with a person who, though quick to anger, immediately seeks a reconciliation once he realizes he has been unjust to another, than with someone who is less easily roused, but also less inclined to seek forgiveness. But *a person who never wants to ask forgiveness, or who fails to do so from the heart* (cf. Matt. 18:35), does not belong in a religious community, even though he may not be sent away.

Be cautious of harsh words. Should you utter them, then do not be afraid to speak the healing word with the same mouth that caused the wound.

3. From time to time the necessity of keeping order may compel you to use harsh words to the young people who have not yet reached adulthood, in order to keep them in line. In that case you are not required to apologize, even though you yourself consider that you have gone too far. For if you are too humble and submissive in your conduct towards these young people, then your authority, which they should be ready to accept, will be undermined. In such cases you should ask forgiveness from the Lord of all, who knows with what deep affection you love your brothers, even those you might happen to have reproved with undue severity. Do not let your love

for one another remain caught up in self-love; rather, such love must be guided by the Spirit.

7 LOVE IN AUTHORITY AND OBEDIENCE

1. *Obey your superior* (Heb. 13:17) as a father, but also give him due respect on account of his office, otherwise you offend God in him. This is even more true of the priest who bears responsibility for you all.

2. It is primarily up to the superior to see that all that has been said here is put into practice and that infringements are not carelessly overlooked. It is his duty to point out abuses and to correct them. If something is beyond his competence and power, he should put the matter before the priest, whose authority in some respects is greater than his own.

3. Your superior must not think himself fortunate in *having power to lord it over you* (Luke 22:25–6), but in *the love with which he shall serve you* (Gal. 5:13). Because of your esteem for him he shall be superior to you; because of his responsibility to God he shall realize that he is the very least of all the brethren. *Let him show himself an example to all in good works* (Titus 2:7); *he is to reprimand those who neglect their work, to give courage to those who are disheartened, to support the weak and to be patient with everyone* (1 Thess. 5:14). He should himself observe the norms of the community and so lead others to respect them too. And let him strive to be loved by you rather than to be feared, although both love and respect are necessary. He

should always remember that *he is responsible to God for you* (Heb. 13:17).

4. By your ready and loving obedience, therefore, you not only *show compassion to yourselves* (Sirach 30:24), but also to your superior. For it applies to you as well that the higher the position a person holds, the greater the danger he is in.

8 CONCLUDING EXHORTATION

1. May the Lord grant that, filled with *longing for spiritual beauty* (Sirach 44:6), you will lovingly observe all that has been written here. Live in such a way that you spread abroad *the life-giving aroma of Christ* (2 Cor. 2:15). *Do not be weighed down like slaves straining under the law, but live as free men under grace* (Rom. 6:14–22).

2. This little book is to be read to you once a week. *As in a mirror, you will be able to see in it whether there is anything you are* neglecting or *forgetting* (James 1:23–5). If you find that your actions match what is written here, thank the Lord who is the giver of every good. If, however, a person sees that he has failed in some way, then let him be sorry for what has occurred in the past and be on his guard for what the future will bring. Let his prayer be: *Forgive me my trespasses and lead me not into temptation* (Matt. 6:12–13).

The Rule of Augustine
(*Feminine Version*)

This text is identical with the masculine text, but
transposed as to gender so that it is appropriate for
communities of women

1 THE BASIC IDEAL: MUTUAL LOVE EXPRESSED IN THE COMMUNITY OF GOODS AND IN HUMILITY

1. We urge you who form a religious community to
   put the following precepts into practice.

2. Before all else, *live together in harmony* (Ps. 67
   (68):7), *being of one mind and one heart* (Acts 4:32) on
   the way to God. For is it not precisely for this reason
   that you have come to live together?

3. Among you there can be no question of personal
   property. Rather, take care that you share everything
   in common. Your superior should see to it that each
   person is provided with food and clothing. She does
   not have to give exactly the same to everyone, for
   you are not all equally strong, but each person should
   be given what she personally needs. For this is what
   you read in the Acts of the Apostles: '*Everything they
   owned was held in common, and each one received whatever
   he or she had need of* ' (Acts 4:32; 4:35).

4. Those who owned possessions in the world should
   readily agree that, from the moment they enter the
   religious life, these things become the property of the
   community.

5. But those who did not have possessions ought not to strive in the religious community for what they could not obtain outside it. One must indeed have regard for their frailty by providing them with whatever they need, even if they were formerly so poor that they could not even afford the very necessities of life. They may not, however, consider themselves fortunate because they now receive food and clothing which were beyond their means in their earlier lives.

6. Nor should they give themselves airs because they now find themselves in the company of people whom they would not have ventured to approach before. Their hearts should seek the nobler things, not vain earthly appearances. If, in the religious life, rich people were to become humble and poor people haughty, then this style of life would seem to be of value only to the rich and not to the poor.

7. On the other hand, let those who appear to have had some standing in the world not look down upon their sisters who have entered the religious life from a condition of poverty. They ought to be more mindful of their life together with poor sisters than of the social status of their wealthy parents. And the fact that they have made some of their possessions available to the community gives them no reason to have a high opinion of themselves. Otherwise people would more easily fall prey to pride in sharing their riches with the community than they would have done if they had enjoyed them in the world. For while all vices manifest themselves in wrongdoing, pride lurks also in our good works, seeking to destroy even them. What good does it do to distribute one's possessions to the poor and to become poor oneself, if giving up riches makes a person prouder than she was when she had a fortune?

8. You are all to live together, therefore, *one in mind and one in heart* (cf. Acts 4:32), and honour God in one another, because *each of you has become his temple* (2 Cor. 6:16).

2 COMMUNITY PRAYER

1. *Persevere faithfully in prayer* (Col. 4:2) at the hours and times appointed.

2. The place of prayer should not be used for any purpose other than that for which it is intended and from which it takes its name. Thus if someone wants to pray there even outside the appointed hours, in her own free time, she should be able to do so without being hindered by others who have no business being there.

3. When you pray to God in psalms and songs, the words spoken by your lips should also be alive in your hearts.

4. When you sing, keep to the text you have, and do not sing what is not intended to be sung.

3 COMMUNITY AND CARE OF THE BODY

1. As far as your health allows, keep your bodily appetites in check by fasting and abstinence from food and

drink. Those who are unable to fast the whole day may have something to eat before the main meal which takes place in the late afternoon. They may do this, however, only around midday. But the sick may have something to eat at any time of the day.

2. From the beginning of the meal to the end listen to the customary reading without noise or protest against the Scriptures, for you have not only to satisfy your physical hunger, *but also to hunger for the word of God* (cf. Amos 8:11).

3. There are some who are weaker because of their former manner of life. If an exception is made for them at table, those who are stronger because they have come from a different way of life ought not to take this amiss or to consider it unfair. They should not think that the others are more fortunate because they receive better food. Let them rather be glad that they are capable of something which is beyond the strength of the others.

4. There are some who, before entering the religious life, were accustomed to living comfortably, and therefore they receive something more in the way of food and clothing: better bedding, perhaps, or more blankets. The others who are stronger, and therefore happier, do not receive these things. But, taking into account the former habits of life of the rich, keep in mind how much they now have to do without, even though they cannot live as simply as those who are physically stronger. Not everyone should want to have the extra she sees another receive, for this is done not to show favour but only out of concern for the person. Otherwise a deplorable disorder would creep into the religious life, whereby the poor begin to drift

easily along while the rich put themselves out in every possible way.

5. The sick should obviously receive suitable food; otherwise their illness would only get worse. Once they are over the worst of their sickness, they ought to be well cared for so that they may be fully restored to health as quickly as possible. And this holds good even if they formerly belonged to the very poorest class in society. During their convalescence they should receive the same that the rich are entitled to because of their former manner of life. But once they have made a complete recovery they are to go back to living as they did earlier on, when they were happier because their needs were fewer. The simpler a way of life, the better it is suited to servants of God.

When a sick person has been restored to health, she will have to be careful not to become the slave of her own desires. She will have to part with the privileges granted because of her illness. Those who have the strength to lead simple lives should consider themselves the richest of people. For it is better to be able to make do with a little than to have plenty.

4 MUTUAL RESPONSIBILITY IN GOOD AND EVIL

1. Do not attract attention by the way you dress. Endeavour to impress by your manner of life, not by the clothes you wear.

2. When you go out, go with somebody else, and stay together when you have reached your destination.

3. Whatever you are doing, your behaviour should in
    no way cause offence to anyone, but should rather be
    in keeping with the holiness of your way of life.

4. When you see a man, do not keep provocatively
    looking at him. Of course, no one can forbid you to
    see men when you go out, *but it is wrong to desire a*
    man or to want him to desire you (cf. Matt. 5:28). For it
    is not only by affectionate embraces that desire
    between man and woman is awakened, but also by
    looks. You cannot say that your inner attitude is good
    if with your eyes you desire to possess a man, for the
    eye is the herald of the heart. And if people allow their
    impure intentions to appear, albeit without words but
    just by looking at each other and finding pleasure in
    each other's passion, even though not in each other's
    arms, we cannot speak any longer of true chastity
    which is precisely that of the heart.

5. Indeed, if a person cannot keep her eyes off a man
    and enjoys attracting his attention, she should not
    imagine that others do not see this. Of course they
    see it; even people you would not expect notice it.
    But even if it did remain concealed and unseen by
    human beings, will it not be seen by *God who scans*
    the heart of every person (Prov. 24:12) and from whom
    nothing is hidden? Or are we to imagine that *God does*
    not see it (Ps. 93(94):7), because just as his wisdom is
    far beyond ours, so too is he prepared to be extraordi-
    narily patient with us? A religious should be afraid *to*
    offend the God of love (Prov. 24:18); for the sake of this
    love she ought to be ready to give up a sinful love
    for a man. Whoever is mindful that God sees all things
    will not wish to look at a man with sinful desire. For,
    precisely on this point, the text of Scripture, '*the Lord*
    abhors a covetous eye' (Prov. 27:20: LXX), impresses
    upon us that we are to stand in awe of him.

6. Therefore, in church or wherever you may be in the company of men, you are to consider yourselves responsible for one another's chastity. Then *God who dwells in you* (2 Cor. 6:16) will watch over you through your responsibility for one another.

7. If you notice in a sister this provocative look I have spoken of, then warn her immediately, so that the evil that has taken root may not worsen and so that she may promptly improve her behaviour.

8. If after this admonition you see her doing the same thing again, anyone who notices it should consider her a sick person in need of treatment. At that time no one is any longer free to be silent. *First inform one or two others of the situation so that with two or three you may be able to convince* her of her fault (Matt. 18:15–17) and to call her to order with due firmness. Do not think that you are acting out of ill-will in doing this. On the contrary, you would be at fault if by your silence you allow your sisters to meet their downfall, when by speaking you could set them on the right path.

Imagine, for example, that your sister had a physical wound which she wanted to conceal for fear of undergoing medical treatment. Would it not be heartless of us to say nothing about it? Rather, would it not be an act of mercy on our part to make it known? How much greater, then, is our obligation to make our sister's condition known and to prevent evil gaining a stronger hold in her heart, something much worse than a physical wound.

9. If she does not wish to listen to your warning, then first advise the superior so that she and the sister may talk the matter out in private, and in this way others will not need to know of it or be involved. If she is

still unwilling to listen, then you may bring in others to convince her of her fault. If she still persists in denying it, then, without her knowledge, others must be brought in, so that her *faults may be pointed out* to her *by more than a single witness in the presence of all* (1 Tim. 5:20), for the word of two or three witnesses is more convincing than that of one.

Once her guilt has been established, it is up to the superior or even to the priest under whose jurisdiction the religious house falls, to determine which punishment she should best undergo with a view to her improvement. If she refuses to submit to this punishment, she is to be sent away from the community, even though she herself may be unwilling to go. Here again this action is not prompted by heartlessness but by love, for in this way she is prevented from having a bad influence on others and contributing to their downfall too.

10.   What I have said about looking at a man lustfully holds too for other sins. In discovering, warding off, bringing to light, proving and punishing all other faults, you are faithfully and diligently to follow the procedure set out above, always with love for the people involved but with aversion for their faults.

11.   If a sister of her own accord confesses that she has gone so far along the wrong path as to receive letters and gifts secretly from a man, we ought to deal with her gently and to pray for her. But if she is found out and proved guilty, she is to be severely punished according to the judgement of the priest or the superior.

5 SERVICE OF ONE ANOTHER

1. Your clothes should be looked after in common by
    one or more sisters who are to see that they are well
    aired and kept free from moths. Just as the food you
    eat is prepared in the one kitchen, so the clothes you
    wear are to come from the one storeroom.

    And, as far as possible, it should not matter to you
    greatly which summer or winter clothes you receive.
    It does not make any difference whether you get back
    the same clothes you handed in or something that has
    been worn by another, *provided no one is denied what
    she needs* (Acts 4:35). If this gives rise to jealousy or
    grumbling, or if people begin complaining that the
    clothes they now have are not as good as those they
    had before, or if they think it beneath them to wear
    clothes that have previously been worn by others,
    does that not tell you something? If the external
    matter of dress becomes a cause of discord, does this
    not prove that inwardly, in the attitude of your heart,
    there is something sadly lacking? But if you are unable
    to do these things and your weakness is taken into
    consideration so that you are allowed to receive again
    the same clothes you handed in, even so, keep them
    all in the one place where they will be looked after
    by those charged with this task.

2. The intention behind all this is that no one will seek
    her own advantage in her work. Everything you do
    is to be for the service of the community, and you
    are to work with more zeal and more enthusiasm than
    if each person were merely working for herself and
    her own interests. For it is written of love that '*it is
    not self-seeking*' (1 Cor. 13:5); that is to say, love puts
    the interests of the community before personal advan-

tage, and not the other way around. Therefore the
degree to which you are concerned for the interests
of the community rather than for your own, is the
criterion by which you can judge how much progress
you have made. Thus in all the fleeting necessities of
human life *something sublime and permanent* reveals
itself, *namely love* (cf. 1 Cor. 12:31; 13:13).

3. It follows from this that a religious who receives
   clothes or other useful items from her parents or relatives may not keep these quietly for herself. She
   should place them at the disposal of the superior. *Once
   they have become the property of the community, it is up
   to the superior to see that these articles find their way into
   the hands of those who need them* (Acts 4:32; 4:35).

4. When you want to wash your clothes or have them
   washed at a laundry, let this take place in consultation
   with the superior lest an exaggerated desire for clean
   clothes sully your character.

5. Because bathing may be necessary for good health,
   the opportunity to visit the public baths may never be
   refused. In this matter follow medical advice without
   grumbling. Even if a person is unwilling, she shall do
   what has to be done for the good of her health, if
   necessary at the command of the superior. But if
   someone wants to go bathing just because she enjoys
   it, when it is not really necessary, she will have to
   learn to renounce her desires. For what a person likes
   may not always be good for her. It may even be
   harmful.

6. In any case, if a sister says that she does not feel
   well, even though she is not noticeably sick, believe
   her without hesitation. But if you are not sure
   whether the treatment she wishes to have will be of
   any benefit to her, then consult a doctor about it.

7.   See to it that there are always two or more of you
     when you visit the public baths. Indeed, this applies
     wherever you go. And it is not for you to choose the
     people who will go with you; you are to leave this to
     the decision of the superior.

8.   Someone should be deputed by the community to
     care for the sick. At the same time this person ought
     to take care of those who are convalescing and those
     who are weak even though they are not running a
     temperature. The infirmarian may take from the
     kitchen whatever she herself considers necessary.

9.   Those responsible for food, clothes and books
     should serve their sisters without grumbling.

10. Books will be available every day at the appointed
     hour, and not at any other time.

11. The sisters in charge of clothes and shoes should
     not delay in making these available to those who need
     them.

6 LOVE AND CONFLICT

1.   Do not quarrel. But if you do have a quarrel, put
     an end to it as quickly as possible. Otherwise an
     isolated moment of anger grows into hatred, *the
     splinter becomes a beam* (Matt. 7:3–5), and you make
     your heart a murderer's den. For we read in the Scrip-
     tures: '*Whoever hates his brother is a murderer*' (1 John
     3:15).

2. If you have hurt a person by abusing her, or by
    cursing or grossly accusing her, be careful to make
    amends for the harm you have done, as quickly as
    possible, by apologizing to her. And the one who has
    been hurt should be ready in her turn to forgive you
    without wrangling. Sisters who have insulted each
    other should *forgive each other's trespasses* (Matt.
    6:12); if you fail to do this, your praying the Our Father
    becomes a lie. Indeed, the more you pray, the more
    honest your prayer ought to become.

    It is better to have to deal with a person who,
    though quick to anger, immediately seeks a reconcili-
    ation once she realizes she has been unjust to another,
    than with someone who is less easily roused, but also
    less inclined to seek forgiveness. But *a person who
    never wants to ask forgiveness, or who fails to do so from the
    heart* (cf. Matt. 18:35), does not belong in a religious
    community, even though she may not be sent away.

    Be cautious of harsh words. Should you utter them,
    then do not be afraid to speak the healing word with
    the same mouth that caused the wound.

3. From time to time the necessity of keeping order
    may compel you to use harsh words to the young
    people who have not yet reached adulthood, in order
    to keep them in line. In that case you are not required
    to apologize, even though you yourself consider that
    you have gone too far. For if you are too humble
    and submissive in your conduct towards these young
    people, then your authority, which they should be
    ready to accept, will be undermined. In such cases
    you should ask forgiveness from the Lord of all, who
    knows with what deep affection you love your sisters,
    even those you might happen to have reproved with
    undue severity. Do not let your love for one another

remain caught up in self-love; rather, such love must be guided by the Spirit.

7 LOVE IN AUTHORITY AND OBEDIENCE

1.   *Obey your superior* (Heb. 13:17) as a mother, but also give her due respect on account of her office, otherwise you offend God in her. This is even more true of the priest who bears responsibility for you all.

2.   It is primarily up to the superior to see that all that has been said here is put into practice and that infringements are not carelessly overlooked. It is her duty to point out abuses and to correct them. If something is beyond her competence and power, she should put the matter before the priest, whose authority in some respects is greater than her own.

3.   Your superior must not think herself fortunate in *having power to lord it over you* (Luke 22:25–6), but in *the love with which she shall serve you* (Gal. 5:13). Because of your esteem for her she shall be superior to you; because of her responsibility to God she shall realize that she is the very least of all the sisters. Let her show herself *an example to all in good works* (Titus 2:7); she is *to reprimand those who neglect their work, to give courage to those who are disheartened, to support the weak and to be patient with everyone* (1 Thess. 5:14). She should herself observe the norms of the community and so lead others to respect them too. And let her strive to be loved by you rather than to be feared, although both love and respect are necessary. She

should always remember that she is *responsible to God for you* (Heb. 13:17).

4.   By your ready and loving obedience, therefore, you not only *show compassion to yourselves* (Sirach 30:24), but also to your superior. For it applies to you as well that the higher the position a person holds, the greater the danger she is in.

8 CONCLUDING EXHORTATION

1.   May the Lord grant that, filled with *longing for spiritual beauty* (Sirach 44:6), you will lovingly observe all that has been written here. Live in such a way that you spread abroad *the life-giving aroma of Christ* (2 Cor. 2:15). *Do not be weighed down like slaves straining under the law, but live as free persons under grace* (Rom. 6:14–22).

2.   This little book is to be read to you once a week. *As in a mirror, you will be able to see in it whether there is anything you are* neglecting *or forgetting* (James 1:23–5). If you find that your actions match what is written here, thank the Lord who is the giver of every good. If, however, a person sees that she has failed in some way, then let her be sorry for what has occurred in the past and be on her guard for what the future will bring. Let her prayer be: *Forgive me my trespasses and lead me not into temptation* (Matt. 6:12–13).

COMMENTARY ON THE
RULE

Commentary on the Rule

1 THE BASIC IDEAL: LOVE AND COMMUNITY

This first chapter contains the basic principles of Augustine's vision of monastic life. Here are to be found the motives, the inspiration and the foundations upon which day-to-day life should be based. The following chapters (2–7) are nothing other than applications and developments of these basic principles for the daily life of a religious community.

The structure of this chapter is as follows:

1 The first community of Jerusalem as the model of a community: of one heart and one mind on the way to God. Live together one in mind and one in heart. Honour God in one another
2 Community of goods as the first realization of life in community
3 Community life is not blind uniformity, but requires the recognition of each person's nature and disposition
4 Humility and pride as positive and negative factors in community life

Live together in harmony*(2)*[1]
In accordance with Augustine's biblical style of writing, various quotations from Scripture are to be found in the very opening words of the Rule. The first is from Psalm 68:7 which, in modern translation, reads: 'God who gives the lonely a home'; but the Latin translation Augustine had before him read: 'God who brings those of one mind together in one house'. It is immediately obvious what a great difference there is between 'the lonely' and 'those of one mind'. The two translations have completely different orientations: loneliness is related to the person as an individual, while being of one mind refers to a group of people. Augustine's intention in quoting this psalm verse is to place all emphasis on community from the beginning.

Being of one mind and one heart*(2)*
In *Sermon* 356 Augustine says: 'How we wish to arrange our life, and how with God's help we are already doing so, is known to many of you from the holy Scriptures. None the less, in order to refresh your memory, the relevant passage from the Acts of the Apostles will be read out. Then you will see where the form of life that we want to practise is described. . . And the deacon Lazarus read: "When they had prayed in this way, the place where they were together shook. They were all filled with the Holy Spirit and confidently proclaimed the word of God to everyone who yearned for the faith. The multitude of believers was of one mind and one heart. And there was no one who called any of his possessions his own property. On the contrary, they owned everything in common" (Acts 4:31–2)'. The first Jerusalem community

---

[1] This figure refers to the paragraph in chapter 1 of the Rule which is being expounded here. Each subsequent figure after a heading indicates in the same way the relevant paragraph in each respective chapter of the Rule.

is the model which Augustine wishes to imitate in his religious community.

Augustine grew towards this ideal; we can trace a development in his thought. In the beginning he gives an explanation of the concept 'of one mind and one heart' which bears precisely the same stamp as the ancient monastic tradition from before his time. Those people are of one mind and one heart who have achieved simplicity of heart by detaching themselves from the stream of temporal, transient things, and who dedicate themselves entirely to God (*Sermon on Psalm 4*, 10). Here it is clearly a matter of the unity within a person as an individual, of inner unity in itself. But, not long afterwards, 'unity of heart' receives another explanation, and this one relates it to community life: the unity among many people. Love for one another then becomes the all-dominating objective: 'through the fire of love they are of one mind and one heart on the way to God' (*Against Faustus* 5, 9).

Augustine has perhaps nowhere put his ideal into words so beautifully as in his *Sermon on Psalm 132 (133)*:

'See how good, how pleasant it is for brothers to live together in unity' (Ps. 133:1) . . . These words of the psalm, this alluring song, this melody pleasant both to the ear and the mind, this has also brought forth the religious communities. Upon hearing this sound, sisters and brothers who desired to live together in unity bestirred themselves. For them this verse was like a trumpet-blast which resounded over the whole earth and brought together those who were divided. It was a cry from God, a cry from the Holy Spirit, a prophetic cry . . . which was heard all over the world. . . The first Christians came from Judaism, and they sold all they owned and laid the proceeds at the feet of the Apostles. They were the first to live together in unity. What then does it mean to live together in unity? The

text of the Acts of the Apostles tells us: 'They were of
one mind and one heart' on the way to God (Acts 4:32).
They were, therefore, the first to hear the words of the
psalm: 'See how good, how pleasant it is for brothers
to live together in unity'. . . Only those in whom love
for Christ is perfect truly live together in unity. For
those in whom love for Christ is not perfect may well
live together, but they are unpleasant, troublesome and
rebellious. In their dissatisfaction they incite others, and
they are always trying to say something unfavourable of
others. They are to be compared with a restive draught-
horse in a team. Not only will it not pull, but with its
hooves it kicks the connecting pole to pieces for good
measure. . . Many sisters and brothers in religious
communities are like this; only to outward appearances
do they live together. But who then truly live together
in unity? Those of whom it is said: 'They were of one
mind and one heart' on the way to God (*Sermon on
Psalm 132*, 2 and 12).

This sermon is important for yet another reason. For
Augustine here gives a very personal explanation of the
word 'monk'. In this word we discover the Greek word
monos which means 'one'. This term belongs to the
vocabulary of the Jewish–Christian morality of simplicity
of heart. Simple persons are those whose hearts are undiv-
ided, who avoid dissipation in their life and activities; they
are of one piece, and they know how to bring unity into
their lives by dedicating themselves totally to the service
of God. This striving for inner unity makes a person a
monk. What Augustine now does is to turn this explanation in the direction of his own ideal of religious
community life. The concept of unity retains its central
place; for him, however, it is no longer in the first instance
a matter of unity within one's own heart, but of unity
with others. Others are to be loved in such a way that

there can no longer be any question of multiplicity, only of unity. The enormous development made here by Augustine is from a personal to an interpersonal interpretation. The community itself should form a strong bond of love, an expression of divine love.

Those who live in unity in such a way that they form but one person are rightly called *'monos'*, one single person. They make true to life what is written, 'of one mind and one heart', that is, many bodies but not many minds, many bodies but not many hearts (*Sermon on Psalm 132*, 6).

From the preceding we are forced to the conclusion that Augustine put his own personal stamp on the religious life. Like all great Christian leaders, he found his inspiration in the Scriptures, particularly in the Acts of the Apostles. Never did he opt for a solitary life. It was always his desire to live out his religious commitment with others in community. His friendly nature was certainly not averse to this. Division and dispersion were for him a denial of love. All his attention is directed to community life, not in itself, but as the practical realization of love. Mutual love flows into the absolute one, the perfect peace, the all-embracing love which God is. 'Together one, in the one Christ, on the way to the one Father' (*Sermon on Psalm 147*, 28) is indeed the shortest summary Augustine ever gave of his ideal.

On the way to God(2)
It is characteristic of Augustine that, to the concept 'of one mind and one heart' from the Acts of the Apostles, he himself almost always adds the words 'on the way to God'. Unanimity as such does not yet make a group a religious community. Unanimity is necessary for the formation of each and every group, whatever its character.

Through the addition of 'on the way to God', however, we are given a good description of what, in Augustine's conception, a religious community is. It is a group of Christians who have decided freely to set out together, united and of one mind and one heart, on the way to God. For this reason, and for this reason alone, have they come together in the first place. From the very beginning, therefore, two features are highlighted: unanimity and being on the way to God. Living together always means striving together; therefore there has to be agreement on the motives for which people form associations, groups or life-communities. This is simply a sociological law. Because people are together on the way to God, the life of the group takes on a religious meaning; it receives an eschatological perspective because it is directed towards God, the ultimate goal of all being. What we are concerned with is a community of believers, or, to express it more pointedly, a faith-community.

This description entails several important consequences. If the important thing is a faith-community, then does the common experience of faith not come before any other objective of a religious group? Does not faith, as the basis upon which the whole enterprise rests, precede every other characteristic, for example an apostolate that might be taken on? Consequently, if we are pilgrims together and share in one another's life of faith, can we then speak of community as a fixed entity in which we can, as it were, establish ourselves? Is entering a religious community not rather to be taken up into a movement? Even as a group we have not yet reached the goal; we are still on the way. It is in any case clear that Augustine does not conceive community as an institution or a structure — anyway, certainly not in the first place — but rather as a network of dynamic relationships between people.

From all this we can draw two important conclusions for the practice of community life:

1 The necessity of a certain agreement or consensus. Community life of whatever kind requires a certain level of concord, harmony, sharing the same ideals and striving towards the same ends. For this reason there have to be definite arrangements with one another which are adhered to as normative, so long as they represent the aspirations of the community and so long as the group recognizes itself in them. If this is lacking, being together is meaningless, as the Rule stresses several times. Being of one mind and one heart on the way to God still has significance for us today. It does not mean that unanimity has to reign on all fronts; what is important is, rather, the sharing of a common inspiration in relation to certain fundamental principles.

2 Sharing in one another's life of faith. For genuine community life, just being side by side together is not sufficient. It is not enough to eat at the same table and to live under the same roof. Interpersonal communication also demands a sharing in one another's inner life, one another's ideas, expectations, longings, activities, hope and faith. This is what Augustine means when he says: 'You live together in the true sense of the word only if you have but one heart' (*Sermon on Psalm 100*, 11).

Community of goods(*3–7*)

Somewhat surprisingly, what follows the exhortation to be of one mind and one heart is the requirement that there be no question of personal property, but that everything must be shared in common. What is the reason for this abrupt transition from such a spiritual ideal to such a material demand? The answer is rather simple: in Augustine's vision, community of goods is the first expression and the first realization of love for one's neighbour.

On this point, too, Augustine's thought underwent development. Voluntary simplicity of life in relation to material goods is like laying aside a burden. Augustine's earliest texts represent this material simplicity as a personal liberation. When a person extricates himself from his attachment to earthly goods in order to follow Christ and to direct his yearning to God as the only true riches, then he becomes a free person. He expressly states this himself: 'But where can we find this perfect simplicity which is absolutely unwavering in unshaken perseverance? In the programme of life that I have already mentioned, namely: "He who does not renounce all that he owns cannot be my disciple" (Luke 14:33). This seems hard, but the word of God flatters no one. Many people have put this into practice. . . Many Jews in Jerusalem sold all that they possessed and laid the proceeds at the feet of the Apostles' (*Sermon Denis* 17, 2–4).

Although the theme of community of goods as liberation is constantly recurring in Augustine, this is not at all his favourite approach. Quite quickly another elucidation becomes more important. Sharing one's possessions is then considered in the perspective of the building up of community with one another; it becomes the expression of relationships among people. It is no longer in the first place a question of an economic decision, nor even of a gesture of detachment. We are concerned, rather, with an attitude to life which wishes to leave behind all self-seeking in order to find happiness in love for the other. At the very centre of things is human community in Christ. In his opusculum *On the Manual Labour of Monks* 25, 32 Augustine puts it as follows:

When a person is converted to the life of a monk, he should not think that he is still doing the same work as he did before. For it is no longer his desire to increase his own possessions, even though they may be very few; his attention is now directed to love of life in community. He now no longer seeks his own interests, but he serves the interests of Jesus Christ. He now lives in the community of those who are of one mind and one heart on the way to God, such that no one can still speak of his own possessions, but all own all goods in common.

Community of goods is for Augustine not merely a condition for love of one another. Sharing goods belongs to the essence of love itself. Love sees to it that whatever each individual has becomes the common property of all. That is the strange power hidden in love: if love is really present, then others own what is mine and I own in others what I do not have in myself. Whoever loves is never completely without possessions. For if a person loves the whole, then everyone who possesses anything has something for him: 'Take envy away, and what I have is yours. Take envy away, and what you have is mine. Possess love, and you possess everything' (*Sermons on John's Gospel* 32, 8). With these words it is by no means Augustine's intention to promote self-love. Love never consciously strives to enrich itself through loving others; that would be a veiled form of self-seeking. Augustine is referring, rather, to a matter of fact: namely, that it is the essence of love to bring about community. Moreover, it is his deepest conviction that, in giving itself, love never diminishes or wanes; on the contrary, through giving itself love grows, and the more people to whom one's love reaches out, the more loving one becomes (cf. *Letter 192*, 1–2).

Augustine applies this line of thought to the religious life. His *Sermon on Psalm 131 (132)*, 3–6 deals with the theme: whoever makes room in himself for love makes room for God in this world:

There are many people who do not want to make a
place for the Lord: they seek only their own interests,
love only what is their own, find their joy in their own
power and strive passionately for their own possessions.
But whoever wants to make a place for the Lord must
seek his joy in the common good and not in his own
possessions. This is precisely what the Christians of
Jerusalem did with their possessions: they made
common possessions of them. Did they thus lose their
own goods? No. If each person owned and held his
own goods for himself alone, then he would have only
his own. But when you share your own goods in
common, then the goods of others become your goods
too.

When Augustine speaks in the Rule of community of
goods, then he intends in the first place material goods.
It would, however, be mistaken to limit the idea of
community of goods to this. It is evident that we ought
also to make our spiritual goods available to one another.
The concept 'spiritual goods' is very broad and difficult
to describe. But it certainly comprises one's own talents,
character, temperament, thoughts and ideas, inspiration
and faith. And even though the first chapter of the Rule
does not explicitly mention it, the sharing of spiritual
goods does indeed seem to be presupposed where Augustine says of religious that, in their dealings with one
another, 'their hearts should seek the nobler things, not
vain earthly appearances'.

We could give the passage of the Rule on community
of goods the classical title of 'the vow of poverty'. We
have, however, avoided this because the word 'poverty'
does not render Augustine's line of thought well. He never
considered poverty, in the sense of a lack of necessary
material goods, as a value in itself. Poverty as deprivation
is never a good thing and has to be combated with all

available forces. Material poverty acquires a positive meaning for Augustine only when it is linked to projects of value, for instance when voluntary poverty is placed at the service of freedom, solidarity and love. Enforced poverty, however, is never a positive thing. Therefore, expressions such as 'community of goods' or 'simplicity of life' are better fitted to the spirituality of Augustine.

Even after these clarifications it is perhaps good to review once again the question as to why the Rule attaches such importance to the sharing of material goods. For Augustine community of goods is clearly very important; in this he faithfully follows his model from the Acts of the Apostles. We moderns could ask ourselves the question whether we do not too easily underrate the material basis of life in community. We are inclined to esteem spiritual integration much more highly than material unity; we would not even be too put out if the latter should just fall away. But are we not then skipping a step? Augustine's reflections on love for one's neighbour start from a very realistic standpoint: love begins from below, love begins with giving, with sharing what we possess. Sharing material goods in common belongs to the first phase of love. This is a first realization of openness towards others, a first form of living together. For, by so doing, we give notice that we no longer wish to live for ourselves or to acquire goods only for our own purposes. Giving up our own possessions has the aim of eliminating our egoism and our selfishness, our craving for domination and power; it is precisely these distorted loves which hinder people from coming together in authentic community. Selfishness keeps us locked up in ourselves; love, on the other hand, makes us break out of the grip of our own ego.

Why is it so difficult for sisters and brothers to be of one heart? Because they are struggling among them-

selves for possession of the earth. . . Sisters and brothers
who wish to live in unity of heart should not let their
love be tied up in the earth. . . They must strive after
possessions that cannot be divided, then they will
always be of one heart. For what is the reason that
discord arises among sisters and brothers? What is it
that interferes with love? All people have indeed come
forth from the one womb. Why, then, are they not of
one spirit? For what other reason than that their spirit
is concentrated upon themselves and everyone is
mindful only of his own share? (*Sermon* 359, 1–2).

It goes without saying that possessions and power are
connected with each other. A selfish person always wants
more, for it is not in the nature of selfishness to say 'that
is enough'. 'If a selfish person has a little cup of water, he
is not satisfied with it; he desires a whole stream' (*Sermon*
50, 4, 6). The struggle for property generally degenerates
into violent conflict; possessing more than others easily
becomes a source of injustice, abuse of power, and repres-
sion (*Sermon on Psalm 38*, 11). All of this prevents people
from truly living together in community.

Voluntarily undertaken simplicity can be lived out in
various ways. To mention just a few forms: a person can
practise simplicity as a process of inner, personal liberation; or as a witness to the world that the divine is the
highest imperishable value in human existence; or as solidarity with others who are doomed out of bitter necessity
to live in privation and dire poverty; or, for example, as
a sharing with one another in order to move forward to
a better society. For Augustine the stress clearly lies on the
last of these: the building up of an authentic community of
love among people. Simplicity for him is at the service of
the building up of true brotherhood and sisterhood among
all.

To each person should be given what he personally needs(3)

Community for Augustine is not the equivalent of uniformity. That everyone must be and receive the same, that all are indistinguishable before the law, that all must wish and not wish the same things: far from being an ideal for Augustine this is obviously a caricature of community life. It is remarkable how much attention is paid in the Rule to the personal differences between the members of the group and with what respect each one's individual personality is approached. The idea of community ought never to lead us to equate people with one another, and to leave it at that. Uniformity reduces people to ciphers and effectively means the destruction of a personality. Love, on the other hand, respects what is characteristic of each person with his different needs and gifts, his own irreplaceable temperament and character. We hear this recurring like a refrain throughout the Rule: do not give the same amount to everyone, but give to each person what he personally needs.

Rich and poor(4-7)

Community life should be so strong that bridges can be built even between opposites. When Augustine speaks here of people who have no possessions and who come from the lowest class of society, he undoubtedly envisages those who served their lord as slaves, or perhaps, still more, impoverished agricultural labourers who hired themselves out for seasonal work. The latter, according to Augustine, were generally in a worse state of insecurity than slaves. Augustine writes in his book *On the Manual Labour of Monks* 22, 25: 'In recent times those coming to this calling in the service of God mostly belong to the class of slaves, either slaves who have already been freed or those who are on the point of being freed by their

masters for this purpose. Others are of peasant stock or
from the working classes or other menial occupations.' On
the other hand, we see that in the religious communities of
that time there were also people from the higher classes
of society who had never had to work for a living and
who were accustomed to being waited upon. The social
problem caused by the immense gulf between the many
poor and the few rich is one of the most prevalent themes
in Augustine's sermons. This affluence of the few was the
cancer of the society of his time. To it he opposes his
religious community as an alternative form of living
together. In such a community it should be possible for
rich and poor, the lowly and the mighty, to relate to each
other as equals and brothers.

Nowadays slavery has been officially abolished. In some
parts of the world – but by no means in all – such sharp
social contrasts perhaps no longer exist. Still, we may not
use this as an excuse for giving scant regard to Augustine's
reflections. It is not difficult to give this principle from the
Rule a broader application. In any group great differences
between people always remain in existence, even if this is
no longer so much the case on the social level. Think, for
example, of the distance between those who have had the
benefit of intellectual formation and those who have not,
or of the difference in temperament between the even-
tempered and the impatient, between passive and active
people, or of the difference between people with difficult
characters and those who are easier to get along with. And
this list could be extended indefinitely. Discrimination
and contempt threaten not only where a difference exists
between rich and poor, but also in all these other cases.
Differences between people ought never in themselves to
become an insuperable barrier to the development of a
healthy society. If we have learnt to share in each other's
talents and have mastered the art of bearing one another's
burdens, then it is possible in normal circumstances to set

up a community in which many differences exist between the members.

Humility and pride*(6–7)*

In the text of the Rule we find a rather unexpected transition to the theme of humility and pride. In Augustine's theology, however, this transition is not at all strange. The connection with the two preceding themes is as follows: (1) first and foremost, religious are to live together of one mind in love; (2) a first expression of this basic principle is the community of goods; (3) now a still more fundamental aspect of living together in love comes up for consideration: namely, humility. For there is no coming to unity without humility, there is no love without the openness of humble patience. 'Where humility reigns, there is love' (*Sermons on the First Letter of John: Prologue*).

For Augustine humility is not just one virtue among others; it is, in the full sense of the word, a basic virtue. All other virtues rest on humility. In this way, humility is also the fertile soil of love. Love's essence is that a person leaves himself in order to go out to another. In love one becomes, as it were, alienated from oneself through the acknowledgement of the other with whom one is face to face. Love therefore compels us to take a distance from ourselves, and this we cannot do without the humility which breaks down the walls imprisoning our ego in itself. In this we see the very important place of humility in Augustine's spirituality. Consider the testimony of the following text:

> I would wish that you place yourself with all your love under Christ, and that you pave no other way in order to reach and to attain the truth than has already been paved by him who, as God, knows the weakness of our

steps. This way is, in the first place, humility; in the second place, humility; in the third place, humility. . . . As often as you ask me about the Christian religion's norms of conduct, I choose to give no other answer than: humility (*Letter* 118, 3, 22).

Pride is the great adversary of humility. All the positive qualities of humility are mirrored negatively in pride. Pride is not simply a fault among other faults, but a basic vice. Augustine describes pride as 'the origin and the beginning of all sins'. Pride and love cannot tolerate each other; indeed, we may say that pride kills love. Therefore, Augustine writes: 'To the extent that we are freed from the malignant swelling which is called pride, we are filled with love' (*On the Trinity* 8, 8, 12). For the proud person is interested only in himself and seeks to have everyone dance to the tune of his own ego.

There is yet another characteristic of pride which is frequently pointed out by Augustine. Here in the Rule he expresses it in the following words: 'All vices manifest themselves in wrongdoing, but pride lurks also in good works, seeking to destroy even them.' What has Augustine in mind here? He means that each vice consists in the doing of some evil: impatience shows itself in quicktemperedness, stubbornness in being unable to admit that one is wrong, dishonesty in deceiving someone, unchastity in the committing of adultery. But the normal vices rest content, as it were, with the performance of the deeds which correspond to their nature. This is not the case with pride. It goes further and meddles also with good deeds in order to corrupt them completely. Pride or self-conceit is a destructive force. A person who boasts of his own qualities and of his own achievements and perfection considers himself better than others. He looks down on others with contempt. Thus, even the good deeds of a proud person lack what is most essential to them: namely,

love. The proud person cherishes an intolerable infatuation
with himself which makes it impossible for him to esteem
others or to relate to them normally. Self-satisfied people
are like ivory towers, closed and inaccessible; they are
impossible to live with. Therefore, Augustine even dares
to assert that 'God's hatred for pride is so strong that he
would rather see humility in evil deeds than pride in good
deeds' (*Sermon on Psalm 93*, 15). In the text of the Rule
too he draws this conclusion when he declares that it is
better to possess a fortune outside the religious
community than to go through life as a proud religious.
He regularly defends this standpoint when he is speaking
of the celibate state of life: 'It is much better to be married
and humble than celibate and proud' (*On Holy Virginity*
51, 52). Thus, we see that the value of religious life ought
not to be exaggerated. In comparison with Christian life
in general, the religious state of life is something relative
and it remains dependent on the highest Christian values
such as love and humility. It is these that are ultimately
decisive and without them the religious life is worthless.

And honour God in one another*(8)*

That the first chapter of the Rule forms a complete unit
in itself is evident from the last sentence, 'You are all to
live together, therefore, one in mind and one in heart, and
honour God in one another', which is a repetition of the
first sentence, 'Before all else, live together in harmony,
being of one mind and one heart on the way to God'. The
phrase 'on the way to God' of the first sentence is changed
here into 'honour God in one another'. We should not
read over this last statement too quickly, for it embodies
a most essential theme of the theology of Augustine:
namely, the identification between love for human beings
and love for God.

When we hear the expression 'to honour God' we are

immediately inclined to think of worship of the divine in the form of prayer, adoration, or meditation, in liturgy, the Eucharist or the other sacraments. But, when he speaks of worshipping God, Augustine thinks in the first place of the love-relationship between people, of loving the sister and brother alongside one. For Augustine the first form of divine worship is to be found in a good community life. This even precedes prayer, to which the Rule comes only in the second chapter. This text of the Rule can best be compared with another text on the religious life which Augustine composed later and which expresses the same theme in different words: 'When brothers and sisters live together in concord, the Lord is praised. For in discord you do not praise the Lord' (*Sermon on Psalm 132*, 13). According to this text too, the praise of God consists primarily in good relationships between community members, and love for other human beings appears as the greatest praise of God.

The Rule says: 'And honour God in one another, because each of you has become his temple.' The theme of God's temple does not turn up accidentally here. For God lives in love. David allowed himself no rest until he had found a place for the Lord, a temple for God to dwell in. Augustine explicates this as follows:

> What can we promise God except that we wish to be his temple? We cannot offer him anything more pleasing than to say to him in the words of Isaiah 26:13: 'Take possession of us' . . . Together all believers form one single place for the Lord. The Lord finds a place in their heart, because all those who are bound together in love have but one single heart. Many thousands of people put their faith into practice by laying the proceeds of their goods at the feet of the Apostles. And what does Scripture say of them? 'They have become the temple of God' (1 Cor. 3:16). Not only did each one individually

become God's temple, but all of them together (*Sermon on Psalm 131*, 3–5).

Only when people become one another's sisters and brothers are they the new temple of God; that is, the place of his presence, for God dwells nowhere but in love. It is not so much the church that is the house of God, but ourselves: 'This church building is the house of our prayers, but we ourselves are the real house of God. Yet, we form together the house of the Lord only if we are joined to one another in love' (*Sermon* 336, 1, 1). God's indwelling comes about both on the personal and the community level: 'For we are his temple, collectively, and as individuals. For he wishes to dwell in the union of all and in each person' (*The City of God* 10, 3).

The background to this way of thinking becomes clear only when we consider that the essence of all divine worship is love. For love is the fulfilment of the Law of Christ. Looked at in this way it is not surprising to perceive that the whole Rule is concentrated upon the relationships of community members among themselves, and that love for God is mentioned explicitly only once (chapter 4). This is absolutely consistent with Augustine's spirituality. In other texts outside the Rule he emphasizes that love for one's neighbour should take precedence over love for God, perhaps not in theory, but certainly in practice. Augustine sees the reason for this in the fact that love for one's neighbour is more concrete and tangible; our relationship to people better enables us to judge whether our love for God is a reality or merely self-deception. We clearly experience our shortcomings with regard to another person; it is not so difficult to know if we have been unjust, unfeeling, dominating or dishonest towards our neighbours. On the other hand, it is much more difficult to experience the authenticity of our love for God. (Cf. *Commentary on the Letter to the Galatians* 45;

Sermons on the First Letter of John 8, 4). For this reason 1 John 4:20 is one of Augustine's favourite verses: 'Whoever does not love his brother whom he sees, cannot love God whom he does not see.'

We can therefore conclude that divine worship consists primarily of love for one another. Prayer, the Eucharist and the sacramental life are not in themselves a sure criterion for judging our love for God. For, without love for people, these become fruitless. For this reason too, in chapter 5 of the Rule, concern for the interests of the community, that is, for the interests of others, is established as the criterion for judging whether we have made progress in love for God. It would, therefore, not be in harmony with the spirituality impressed upon us by the Rule if we were to be suspicious of human relationships, or to regard them as inferior, or to be of the opinion that love for other human beings can stand in the way of love for God. The two loves are not competing with each other, but they embrace each other in one great dynamic movement. Of course, all of this is valid only of genuine love; for not everything that is called love is really love. Augustine himself warns us with the following words:

> Sisters and brothers, if you want to live in love, then first be aware that love is no trifling matter; it is not something cheap and easy for which nothing has to be done. One lives in love not just by being good-humoured. Actually, this is putting it too mildly. To be more precise, the lazy, the indifferent and the non-chalant are not living in love. Do not think that you love your servant just because you refrain from striking him, or that you love your child if you do not bother to teach him discipline, or that you love your neighbours if you never speak to them. That is not love, but weakness (*Sermons on the First Letter of John* 7, 11).

Love must have the well-being of the other in view; it ought not to be an unconscious projection of ourselves. This means that we never have the right to use others by having them serve us. That would lead to the destruction of the other person. But this maxim can equally well be applied to the community: one ought not to use the community for oneself, for it is essential to community that it be made up of living persons.

2 PRAYER AND COMMUNITY

This small chapter is devoted almost entirely to community prayer. Only the third sentence has to do with individual prayer.

Structure of this chapter:

1 Fixed times for community prayer
2 Opportunity for individual prayer
3 The basic law of all prayer
4 Practical norms for the singing of psalms and hymns

Persevere faithfully in prayer(1)
Faithful perseverance in prayer at appointed hours and times is a necessary requirement for a faith-community. Regular prayer can be threatened in various ways, for instance when we allow our prayer to depend on whether we are in the mood to pray or not, or when we no longer make time free for prayer because we are overburdened by work. Augustine speaks from experience when he writes: 'If it were up to me to choose, I would much rather perform some manual work at certain hours each

day, as these are laid down in well-run religious communities, so as to have the rest of the time free to read, to pray, or to study one or other book of the holy Scriptures. I would much prefer to do this than to have to sit through the turbulent and confused court cases of people I do not know' (*On the Manual Labour of Monks* 29, 37).

The place of prayer(2)

That the place of prayer be used for no purpose other than prayer is probably related to the rather limited living space of Augustine's first foundations. We know, for example, that the monastery at Tagaste, founded towards the end of the year 388, was really nothing more than Augustine's family house. Because of lack of space then, it could easily happen that the oratory, outside the hours of community prayer, would be taken over for other purposes. Augustine wants to prevent this happening so as to give everyone the opportunity for individual prayer.

The basic law of all prayer(3)

The essence of the Rule's teaching on prayer is to be found in the sentence: 'When you pray to God in psalms and songs, the words spoken by your lips should also be alive in your hearts.' This, according to Augustine, is the basic law of all prayer. There has to be harmony between lips and heart, between the exterior and the interior, between theory and practice, the ideal and life. The possibility of disharmony in the human person is always present, for how easily a gulf can open up between what we appear to be and what we really are. Our prayer should be part of our deepest selves; our life should witness to our ideal.

We wish to clarify this by looking at several other texts of Augustine on the same theme. In answer to the question why we ought to use words too in order to speak to God, he states: 'With regard to this question, I would like first of all to reply that we should not use words to parley with God in order to receive what we desire; our conversation with God should rather focus on what we bear in our hearts, on the attention of our spirit, on a pure love and honest yearning. It is with words that our Lord has taught us these essential things; and, at the time of prayer, these words committed to our memory put us in mind of the essentials' (*On the Lord's Sermon on the Mount* 2, 3, 13). Here we find the reason why we should also pray with words, even though prayer at its deepest is more than words. The essence of prayer is to be sought at the heart of Jesus' message, and that means in faith, hope and love. When we really believe, hope and love, then there springs up in us a deep yearning which, according to Augustine, is at the heart of all true prayer. The attitude of a prayerful person is the same as that of one who desires and longs. 'Longing is always at prayer, even though the tongue is silent. If your yearning is constant, then you are always praying. When does our prayer sleep? Only when our desire cools' (*Sermon* 80, 7). But once again, even though the prayer of the heart is the most important, this does not make verbal prayer superfluous. 'In faith, hope and love we are praying always with uninterrupted longing. But at particular hours and times we entreat God also with words so that, through these verbal signs of the reality, we may impel ourselves to greater effort, help ourselves become aware of how much progress we have made in this desire, and rouse ourselves to grow in it with greater vitality. . . Therefore, at certain times, we call our spirit back to prayer from the other cares and activities which in some way cloud our yearning' (*Letter* 130, 9, 18). Keeping these texts before us we shall be quite clear what Augustine means when he speaks in the Rule of the harmony of word and heart.

Practical norms*(4)*

It is not easy to interpret the two practical norms given by the Rule. We have too little information about the concrete circumstances to which they refer. The words 'when you sing, keep to the text you have' are most probably to be related to the many different translations of the Bible that were then in circulation.

We have to try to imagine the situation somewhat as follows. The Old Testament was originally written in Hebrew, and various Greek translations were later made. One of these, the so-called Septuagint translation, enjoyed unarguable authority in East and West. This Septuagint translation was in its turn the basis for numerous Latin translations which were quite different from one another. At that time there were as yet no Latin translations which went back to the original Hebrew text. Jerome would be the first to set to work on a translation of this kind. At the time of Augustine, however, almost every Western church province had its own translation of the Scriptures and it would be many years before a universally accepted translation would more or less win through. Augustine came into conflict with Jerome over the matter of the new translation of the Old Testament which was being made on the basis of the original Hebrew text and which was designed to replace all other Latin translations. Augustine was not opposed in principle to a new translation, but for practical and pastoral reasons he preferred the traditional Latin translations based on the Septuagint. Because the Septuagint was regarded so highly in the Eastern churches, Augustine feared that a break would occur between East and West if the West were to deviate from the Septuagint. The bishop of Hippo therefore wanted, in so far as possible, to respect the various traditional Latin translations of the Septuagint, and, in this way, he was indirectly a proponent of the pluriformity of Bible translations. We think therefore that the words 'keep to the text you have' may be interpreted as follows: keep to the text of the Scriptures which it is customary to read in the place where you are.

'And do not sing what is not intended to be sung.' This may be a reaction against the tendency of the North Africans to repeat songs endlessly and to draw them out *ad nauseam*; but we cannot be certain. In *Letter* 55, 18, 34 there is some indication that this may be the case: Augustine refers to the fact that there are different manners of singing and that the Catholics of North Africa are accustomed to practise self-control in their singing, something for which they are reproached by the Donatists. This self-control is undoubtedly to be related to Augustine's attitude towards sacred music in general as he describes it in his *Confessions* 10, 33, 50. He is apprehensive lest the aesthetic pleasure too greatly distract his attention from the meaning of the text that is sung. Not without reason, he fears that the enjoyment of beauty and genuine prayer can come into conflict with each other. Yet he affirms – without wishing to make an irrevocable statement – that he feels rather inclined to defend the custom of singing in church, because our frail spirit can more easily be stirred to love by the beauty of song. He does not wish, however, to be more moved by the singing than by what is sung. Perhaps this text from the *Confessions* provides sufficient points of contact to explain Augustine's concern for self-control in singing as this is expressed in the Rule.

3 COMMUNITY AND CARE OF THE BODY

The main theme of this chapter is care for the weaker and sick brothers and sisters. We as a group ought to be concerned for one another's health.

Structure of this chapter:

1 Moderation in eating and drinking
2 Reading during meals
3 Difference in treatment according to the person in question (on this point too, respect for the uniqueness of each person)
4 Care of the sick

Fasting*(1)*

The text begins with a call to personal asceticism in the matter of food and drink. For Augustine, asceticism means denying oneself something which is lawful, with the intention of strengthening oneself, so that one is able to offer resistance to disordered desires and to avoid becoming prey to longings for the unlawful (*Sermon* 207, 2). It is remarkable how few severe, ascetical elements are to be found in the Rule. This reference to fasting is almost the only one. The strict asceticism common in most monastic milieus at the time is foreign to Augustine. From the *Life of Augustine* written by his friend Possidius we know that Augustine was very moderate when it came to ascetical practices: there was always wine at table, and it was Augustine's expressed wish that silver spoons be used at meals; the rest of the tableware was of stone, wood or marble (Possidius, *Life of Augustine* 22). The absence of rigid ascetical practices as such has undoubtedly to be seen in the light of the fact that the common life in itself demands great asceticism. Moreover, for Augustine, it is not a matter of austerity for austerity's sake; that is, as mere training in self-control. The goal of asceticism extends further than this. In fact, others must be advantaged by our acts of self-denial. As Augustine repeatedly points out, there is no value in fasting unless one gives to the poor what is thereby saved (*Sermon* 209, 2).

In order to understand the text of the Rule on fasting we have to take the eating customs of that time into account. The first meal of the day – we would call it breakfast – was taken towards midday, while the main meal took place between three and five in the afternoon. What fasting entailed was skipping breakfast and waiting until the time of the main meal before having anything to eat. Augustine's caution in making these recommendations to fast, however, is clearly apparent from the three limiting conditions which are summed up in the Rule at this point: (1) 'as far as your health allows': health is obviously more important than asceticism; (2) an exception is also made for those who are not able to do without food for the whole day, that is, until after three in the afternoon; these may eat twice a day, first towards midday and later at the main meal after three; (3) finally, the sick enjoy a general dispensation from the obligation to fast; their sickness is in itself a sufficient trial.

Reading at table(2)

According to the Rule, it was the custom that someone read aloud at table. The purpose of this will certainly have been to instruct the members of the community. We may assume that some of them would not have had the aptitude for independent study; through the reading at table they were nourished by the word of God. It is questionable, however, whether there was always reading during meals in Augustine's religious communities. For we read in Possidius' *Life*: 'At table Augustine had a greater liking for the reading and the conversation than for food and drink' (*Life of Augustine* 22). Conversation at table was evidently not excluded.

Normally it would have been the Scriptures that were read. This follows from the reference to the words of the prophet Amos 8:11: 'See what days are coming – it is the

Lord Yahweh who speaks – days when I will bring famine to the country, a famine not of bread, a drought not of water, but a hunger and thirst to hear the word of Yahweh.' Augustine here once again makes his familiar transition from the external to the inward, from physical hunger to the hunger of the heart. The text of Amos offers him a splendid opportunity for it.

When we read in the Rule 'listen to the customary reading without noise or protest', it strikes us as rather strange. But we have to take into account here the excitable temperament of the North African. He would not have listened impassively as we might, but had the habit of interrupting the speaker by bursting out in expressions of approval or disapproval. Often, when the Scriptures were read at table, the listeners felt an urge to comment out loud, to put questions or to raise objections. Also, in his *Commentary on the Sermon on the Mount* 1, 4, 11 Augustine exhorts his hearers to listen to the Scriptures with tranquillity and openness, respect and reverence; they are not to criticize the Scriptures because they find something there which they do not understand, and they are not to oppose them out of obstinacy.

Respect for the person(3–5)

The remainder of this chapter is again devoted to the respect that is to be shown for the uniqueness of each person. In the case of two particular groups of people exceptional treatment is provided for: they are those who are weaker because of their former manner of life, and consequently also the sick. It is not that certain persons are privileged; it is, rather, a matter of respect for the differences in disposition between persons. The difference in the way individuals are treated because they are physically stronger or weaker than others should not be a source of envy or jealousy, of vexation or false accusations. This

is so even if the weakness of some is the result of their
less hardy upbringing or of their life-style before they
entered the religious community. The weak person is not
better off because his needs are greater. On the contrary,
those who are stronger are in fact more fortunate. For
they are capable of doing more and they need less. What
is meant here by 'more fortunate' or 'happier' is that a
person is blessed by God with natural gifts and abilities
such as health, the capacity for work, and staying-power.
Not everyone is in a position to emulate the attainments
of others, but, if each person attains what is within his
reach, then a balance is struck. Therefore everyone is
summoned to do what he can. When this does not happen,
the life of the community degenerates into a hotbed of
disorders: some put themselves out and make great efforts,
while others just drift along taking the line of least resistance. Augustine expressed the same idea in a very telling
manner in his *Letter* 130, 16, 31 to the widow Proba and
her circle:

> Each of you must do what she can. If one person is not
> capable of as much as another, then she can still attain
> it in the other who does have this capability. The condi-
> tion is that she love and esteem in the other the attain-
> ments which she herself does not have because in herself
> she is incapable of them. Thus the person with fewer
> capabilities ought not to impede the person with more;
> and nor should those who are more gifted put pressure
> on others who are capable of less. You have to render
> an account of your conscience to God alone. But the
> only thing that you owe one another is love for one
> another (Rom. 13:8).

The sick should find themselves in an environment of
the greatest care. They ought to be treated as rich people.
In other words, the attention that they receive is to be in
no way inferior to the care which the rich could afford

before they entered the religious life or to the treatment which the rich still enjoy in the community because of their former manner of life. None the less, the person who has been sick should be on his guard lest he become too attached to the preferential treatment he enjoyed during his illness. For the capacity to live simply is a sign of inner grandeur.

It is better to be able to make do with little than to have plenty*(5)*

In these words Augustine reproduces a widespread religious and philosophical ideal: inner freedom is to be preferred to material possessions. We would not be seeing far enough into his intention if we were to read in these words nothing more than a warning against possessing too much, against excessive or unjustly acquired possessions. For Augustine takes up a more radical position. It can be stated roughly as follows: a person can be happier in lacking something than in possessing it. Why? Because someone with many needs and wants will be continuously haunted by the craving for more. Such a person can never find rest and is never contented. Note well: Augustine is not making a plea for material poverty, as if want in itself could make a person happy. Rather, the object of his attack is the tyranny of need, and he wants to convince people to overcome selfishness.

We could, however, object: are our longings and desires not satisfied if we effectively possess what we have longed for and desired? Augustine will have no hesitation in answering this question in the negative. Generally speaking, the more a person has, the more he desires to have. Rich people are mostly in want because of their desire to possess more and more. Therefore, to desire less means to be less in need, less poor, not in a material sense but in a spiritual sense. Consequently, for Augustine,

voluntary religious poverty involves not only the relinqui-
shing of material goods but also of the desire for them.
Otherwise, voluntary simplicity of life will not be accompanied by an inner liberation. 'To leave the whole world
behind: this means to relinquish what you have and what
you wish to have' (*Letter* 157, 4, 39). The inner freedom
that this brings expresses itself in yet another way, for it
is evident that a person who has great possessions also
has much more trouble and worry than someone whose
possessions are few. A rich person has, for example, to
take measures to protect and to preserve his property,
while a person who is contented with little is a stranger
to such cares. Such a person is in fact better off; he is
richer.

For Augustine, earthly goods are not bad in themselves.
Silver and gold are not themselves unjust, but the person
who makes use of them for unloving ends. Silver and
gold represent a call to mercy and humanity. But, for the
selfish person, they are a goad to greediness. Thus people
chase madly after earthly goods, but in vain, for such
goods can never ultimately measure up to a person's inner
need. On the contrary, material riches frequently leave
behind a burning need to acquire more and more. Such
riches are false; they do not bring contentment, but only
arouse craving. 'We notice that people who have little
money are happy when they make just a small profit. But
when abundance comes their way – a vast amount of silver
and gold – they refuse the small things that are offered to
them. You may think that they do this because they are
satisfied with what they already have; but that is not the
case. For money, no matter how much, does not close
the jaws of selfishness but opens them more widely still.
Greater possessions do not slake people's thirst but
increase it. Such people despise a small cup of water
because they want to have a whole stream' (*Sermon* 50, 4,

6). Thus our conclusion is: consider as rich the person
who is least consumed by the desire for material goods.

4 MUTUAL RESPONSIBILITY FOR ONE
ANOTHER

The unmarried state of life, celibacy, or, in modern terms,
the vow of virginity, form the background to this chapter.
In the monastic world of Augustine's time, that a person
would remain unmarried was presupposed as self-evident.
This also seems to be the case in the Rule. In contrast to
what the Rule has to say about poverty and obedience, it
does not in fact give a positive description of virginity.
For a more positive and personal vision of virginity in
Augustine we have to look to his later works, although
even there we must keep in mind that, as far as the
man–woman relationship is concerned, Augustine remains
a child of his time. Here in the Rule, however, it is exclusively a matter of transgressions against virginity. Therefore we could as well give this chapter the title: on our
mutual responsibility in evil.

Structure of this chapter:

1 General norms for irreproachable conduct
2 Irreproachable conduct and one's inner attitude
  towards those of the other sex
3 Common responsibility for one another's faults
4 This responsibility must be expressed in correction
5 Procedure to be followed in correcting others
6 This manner of acting holds also as the model for
  the correction of other faults

Dress, and attitude towards the outside world *(1–3)*
Nowhere do we find in Augustine's works that a special
form of dress existed for religious. Their clothing seems
to have been that worn by the lower classes. One should
dress simply: clothes make not the man; rather, our attitude towards life makes us what we are. God does not
seek a handsome appearance, but a good heart. Elsewhere
in his works Augustine makes the connection between
simplicity in dress and moral modesty: avoid dressing too
elegantly out of a desire to be noticed or to please (*On
Holy Virginity* 34, 34). We should not think that Augustine's remarks on dress are intended only for women.
Possidius records for us Augustine's own attitude: 'His
clothing and footwear were modest, but fitting, neither
too refined, nor too shabby or slovenly' (*Life of Augustine*
22). And in *Sermon* 356, 13 we hear Augustine himself
affirm:

> Give what you will. From the gifts made to the
> community each person will receive what he needs. . .
> I too receive from community property, and whatever
> goods I have I wish to have only as belonging to the
> community. Therefore I do not want you to bring gifts
> which I alone can use because, so to speak, they are
> more appropriate to my standing. If, for example,
> someone were to give me a costly garment, it may well
> be the thing for a bishop, but not for Augustine. For
> he is a poor man and a child of poor parents. Otherwise
> people would soon be saying that I have received expen-
> sive clothes such as I could never have had in my
> parental home or if I had pursued a profession in the
> world. That would not be proper. My clothes should
> be such that I can also give them to my brother if he is
> without. I will accept clothes that can be worn by
> priests, deacons and sub-deacons, because I accept them
> for the community. If someone gives me better clothing

than this, then I sell it. . . I sell it and give the money
to the poor. . . Yes, I admit that I am ashamed to wear
expensive clothing, because it is not in keeping with
my religious state of life.

The Rule's precept about not going out alone has to be
understood in the context of life in a different time and
culture. It is intended as a kind of protection and is to be
seen in the light of the rather enclosed character of religious communities of former times. In today's society this
regulation has become impossible to keep. This does not
mean, however, that it has nothing more to say to us.
But it is meaningful now in a different way; for example,
if someone is absent for a lengthy period and no one
knows where he is, then this is a sign of a poor sense of
community and openness to one another.

Attitude towards persons of the other sex *(4–11)*
This whole passage on provocative staring at a person of
the other sex has to be read in the light of Matthew 5:27–8:
'You have learnt how it was said: "You must not commit
adultery". But I say this to you: if a man looks at a woman
lustfully, he has already committed adultery with her in
his heart.' It is not a question here of ordinary contact
between persons of different sexes; it is, rather, a matter
of the desire or the craving to possess one another sexu-
ally. Such desire expresses itself in the eye, for the eye is
the herald of the heart. Basing himself on the text of
Matthew, Augustine makes a distinction between the
value of our senses and the evil of lust; the use of our
sight is of course something good, but to use our sight
for evil purposes is quite another matter. What Augustine
really means by lust is the fundamental decision for evil
(*Uncompleted Work against Julian* 4, 29; *On the Lord's Sermon
on the Mount* 1, 12, 33). Matthew 5:27–8 once again offers

Augustine an opportunity to make a transition from the outward to the inward, from the violation of virginity by physical acts to the unfaithfulness of the heart. It is first in the human heart that our actions are formed, because from our hearts emerge all our deeds (cf. Mark 7:21).

Making use of Proverbs 24:12, 'He who scans the heart knows everything about it', Augustine points out that nothing can remain hidden from God whose patience with human beings is as great as his wisdom. Two biblical themes – those of God's wisdom and his patience – are here linked together. The former we find expressed in Jesus Sirach 15:18–19: 'For vast is the wisdom of the Lord; He is almighty and all-seeing. His eyes are on those who fear him, every human action is known to him'; the latter in Wisdom 12:10: 'But, by punishing them patiently piece by piece, you gave them the chance to repent.' This association of themes leads Augustine to the reflection that, because God's wisdom is greater than that of human beings, so too is his patience. People are quick to condemn, but this is often a sign of unwisdom. An over-hasty condemnation drives a person who has committed some fault into even deeper trouble; it deprives him of all hope and diminishes his chances of picking himself up again. The wiser a person is, the deeper is his awareness of his own weakness, and the more patient he becomes with the other. This is true to a much greater extent of God: his patience is the reverse side of his wisdom. In the background here is also the text of Romans 2:4: 'Or are you abusing his abundant goodness, patience and generosity, not realizing that this goodness of God is meant to lead you to repentance?' According to Augustine, God's patience testifies to his wisdom on two counts, for he is patient with the intention both of bringing sinners to conversion and of giving a warning to good people by letting them see the destruction which evil wreaks.

Responsibility for one another(6)

As we know, the primary concern of Augustine in his Rule is the relationships within the community. Here once again the same trend is evident. He is thinking not so much of each person's individual responsibility, but of the responsibility of the group as a whole. The emphasis is not so much on my responsibility for myself as on my responsibility for others. The words, 'God who dwells in you will watch over you through your responsibility for one another' do not refer directly to the indwelling of God in individual people – although Augustine is certainly not unfamiliar with this idea – for the 'in you' is in the plural. Because of its plural form the 'in you' has to be understood as meaning: God who lives in your community, in all of you together. The other expression, *ex vobis*, which we have translated 'through your responsibility for one another', is also obviously plural. Thus the stress once again comes to lie on the community. Consequently, what Augustine means is this: God watches over us from within the community, through the people around us. This is the reason for the translation 'God will watch over you through your responsibility for one another'. God watches over us, but not without our help; he watches over us through others. No one can say: what have I to do with you, let each one look after himself. The community bears the responsibility for the good and the evil of each of its members.

God takes care of us through others: this was our conclusion after having examined the text of the Rule. We find confirmation for this conclusion in a canon of the Council of Hippo from the year 393, where exactly the same idea occurs. The bishops at that Council were responding to the situation of women who had taken the vow of virginity but who lived alone. It needs to be pointed out that, for a long period in the early Church, it was the custom for women who had committed themselves to virginity either to remain living in the parental home or to live on their own in society. The Council of Hippo wanted to effect a change in this situation, for it was worried that, once these women were no longer in the care of their parents but living all on their own, loneliness might put the success of their consecrated way of life drastically at risk. The Council calls on them to live together and to watch over one another. Thus a strong plea is made for community life: 'That consecrated virgins, whose parents are no longer in a position to watch over them, either be entrusted to responsible women by the direction of the bishop or the priest, or watch over each other living together in the same house, so that they do not bring the good name of the Church into disrepute by running around everywhere.' Therefore, both in the Rule and in this North African Council, community life is considered as a protection for a person's faith commitment. The meaning of community life is, among other things, that a person in a group is capable of more than if he were left entirely to his own resources. In the realm of faith the social nature of the human person cannot be ignored; this is a truth which is still well worth pondering.

Correction *(7–10)*

One of the forms which responsibility for one another can take is warning or reprimanding a person who finds himself on the wrong path. The procedure to be applied in such cases is this:

1 First of all, the person at fault is to be warned by the person who has noticed it.
2 Then, the one charged with responsibility for the community is to be called in.
3 Later, a number of people should be informed of the situation.

4   Finally, the transgressor's faults are to be pointed out
to him or her in the presence of the whole community.

In this, Augustine is following a very old tradition
concerning the organization of religious communities. We
find this same tradition in Matthew 18:15–17: 'If your
brother does something wrong, go and have it out with
him alone, between your two selves. If he listens to you,
you have won back your brother. If he does not listen,
take one or two others along with you: the evidence of
two or three witnesses is required to sustain any charge.
But if he refuses to listen to these, report it to the church
community; and if he refuses to listen to the church
community, treat him like a pagan or a tax collector.'
In Matthew the procedure progresses in three phases: a
personal warning; two or three witnesses; the whole
community. Augustine makes one alteration to this way
of dealing with matters: he assigns a role also to the leader
of the community, such that the procedure now includes
an extra phase. The one charged with responsibility for
the religious community is to invite the person who has
acted wrongly for a private talk. This is done in order to
protect the good name of the wrongdoer for as long as
possible. Only in the third phase may the wrong which
has been done be made known to a wider circle of people,
and then only if there are no signs of improvement. This
expansion of the procedure is probably the reason why
the procedure itself is mentioned twice in quick succession
in the Rule: first in the form which was customary in the
early Christian church community (Matt. 18:15–17), and
then in its application to a religious community. In all that
has been said up to now, one should not lose sight of the
fact that correcting the wrongdoer is not a matter for the
superior alone, but rather a task for the whole group.

If someone refuses to acknowledge that he has done
wrong, and if he keeps denying all guilt and shows no

sign of willingness to improve his behaviour, then he must be punished. At this stage the intention of the punishment is to help the wrongdoer even now to see the error of his ways. If, however, the person refuses to submit to the punishment he is given, the community then has the right to send him away, for otherwise the ideal of the whole group may be exposed to danger. Ridding the group of those who openly flout its ideal is really a kind of self-defence.

If we find this too strict, then we must keep in mind that engaging in religious life is always a question of free choice. It is noticeable how Augustine shows greater tolerance in bearing with wrongdoers in the Church than with those in a religious community. Of course, a religious community too should be able to muster a certain measure of forbearance towards its own weak members. Augustine emphasizes this often enough. For him, however, forbearance in a religious community is not to go to the same lengths as that tolerance required of the Church in relation to its sinful members. Because Augustine regards the Church as being in the first place an invitation to the Kingdom of God addressed to all kinds of people, strong and weak, good and bad, therefore he considers tolerance within the Church as almost limitless. And the ultimate judgement over good and evil is reserved to God alone. It is not given to human beings to determine with certainty the boundary between good and evil. Therefore only God can in the last instance define the borders of his Kingdom. Based on these principles, Augustine's position on who belongs to the Church is most cautious and generous.

When it comes to a religious community, however, we no longer meet this same leniency; Augustine is stricter in this matter. This is not the only reference in the Rule to sending somebody away; in chapter 6, too, Augustine speaks plainly of people who, because they are never willing to ask forgiveness, do not belong in a religious community. The reason for this greater strictness is clearly related to the difference between the church community and a religious community. The Church is a much more indispensable means of salvation than a religious community. The moral obligation to belong to the church community is therefore much greater than any obligation to become part of a religious community. No one is under an obligation to enter the religious life in order to gain his salvation. There is then much more at stake when a person leaves the church community than when someone leaves a religious community. Moreover, the freedom to become a member of the Church differs from the freedom with which one enters a religious community. The fact that we belong to the Catholic Church is to some extent (but to a not unimportant extent) determined by who our parents happened to be, by the country in which we were born, by the culture in which we were immersed from infancy, by the education we received. All of this, as it were, created an environment in which the encounter with Jesus cannot go wrong. There is therefore a greater determinism involved in membership of the Church than in being a member of a religious community. One's choice for the latter is based more on one's own initiative and free will. Religious life is a freely chosen ideal. But the ideal can only exist thanks to idealists, and only thanks to an enduring free commitment does a person remain a religious. If freedom and idealism disappear, religious life loses all sense and meaning. Therefore it is not at all surprising that Augustine is stricter with regard to membership of a religious community than with regard to membership of the Church.

Superior–priest *(9–11)*

Here we are given a glimpse into the structure and constitution of Augustine's monastic foundations. In his communities there is evidently a twofold authority, that of the superior and that of the priest. In order to understand this properly, we have to recall that, in the early Church, religious life originated as a lay-movement. We encounter this lay-character also in Augustine's foundations. His first community at Tagaste, founded in 388, was a community of lay-people. The same holds for his first foundation at Hippo in 391, even though he himself was then already a priest. When, however, Augustine was ordained bishop in 395/396, he still wished to continue living in a religious community, and therefore he founded a second monastery in Hippo, this time for clerics (that is, deacons, priests and bishops).

The text of the Rule reflects the situation of Augustine's original foundations. At the head of the community is a lay-superior (*praepositus*) who presides over the day-to-day running of the community. Alongside him is a priest. The priest's task is not to provide leadership for the group in all its aspects; rather, he is competent exclusively in matters pertaining to the proclamation of the faith and the sacramental life of the community members. It is in this light too that we are to understand the words of chapter 7: 'If something is beyond the competence and power of the superior, he should put the matter before the priest. . .'

Healing of wounds *(8)*

The deeper aim of correction is to set in motion the process of healing. If someone sees what is wrong and yet does nothing about it, he is acting without love. When a person is concerned for the good of his fellow human beings, he cannot just stay quiet and allow evil to run rampant: 'Do you scorn your brother's wound? You see him heading for destruction, or perhaps he has already been destroyed, and you do nothing? Because you remain silent, you are worse than he is when he curses you' (*Sermon* 82, 4, 7).

When a physical wound is taken care of, everyone experiences it as a boon. Why should it be different in the case of a spiritual wound? Here too Augustine once again makes his well-known transition from bodily reality to the human heart. There is no one who has any doubt that he is doing another a service when he puts a person with a tumour or an open wound under pressure to have medical treatment. And if he fails to convince the person of this in private conversation, then he will take others into his confidence so as to get the suffering person to change his mind and to decide to seek medical advice. Everyone naturally recoils from the pain that surgery involves, but the only aim of surgery is the health of the patient. It would be irresponsible to keep quiet about the ailment only because the patient is afraid. This theme appears very often in Augustine's works. For example, we read in *Sermon* 83, 7, 8:

> Let us correct one another. . . When the Lord says 'You must forgive your brother from the heart' (Matt. 18:35), he did not add the words 'from the heart' for nothing. For, when we take disciplinary measures, gentleness ought not to fade from our hearts. Indeed, who is more loving than a physician with a surgical knife in his hand? Of course, the person who has to undergo the operation weeps. But the surgeon's treatment is not cruel; we would not think of calling it harsh. Certainly, the doctor is harsh on the wound, but only in order to heal the person. For, if he were too gentle on the wound, the human being would perish.

If this is true with regard to physical evil, it is equally true with regard to the spiritual evil which afflicts the human heart. Correction is to be compared with medical treatment; it is indeed painful, but its only aim is the restoration of health. This does not mean to say that Augustine was completely uncritical of the practices of correction and punishment. He was too gentle a character not to shudder at the murky aspects tied up with any intervention in the life of another. The following text shows this clearly:

> What am I to say about punishing and not punishing? For it is obviously our wish that whatever we do should redound completely to the good of those whom we think we have to punish or not to punish. What measure of punishment is called for, not only in relation to the nature and the seriousness of the offence, but also in relation to a person's spiritual strength? How much can a person stand? Are there not punishments a person will baulk at, such that not only will he derive no advantage from them, but he will also collapse under their severity? What deep dark questions! . . . I do not know either how many people have become better because of punishment or how many have turned out worse on its account. And what is one to do in the case that frequently presents itself: if you punish a certain person, he is lost; if you allow his wrongdoing to go unchecked, another person is corrupted by it? . . . Paulinus, holy man of God, terror strikes my heart when I think of all these matters. What darkness! (*Letter* 95, 3).

Love for the person; aversion for his faults(10)

This too is a theme that recurs many times in Augustine's works. How easily it can happen that we reject someone because of his faults. In order to avert this, Augustine constantly makes a distinction between the person and his faults. Thus he writes in *Letter* 153, 1, 3:

> It is easy and requires no effort to hate the wicked because they are wicked. But it is exceptional and good to love them because they are human beings. Then, in one and the same person, you disapprove of his offence and, at the same time, approve of his human nature. And the more justified you are in hating the offence, the greater the love you have for the human nature deformed by it. The person who loves in this way persecutes wickedness, but his sole intention in doing so is to free the human being affected by this wickedness. Such a person is not shackled by any bond with wickedness itself; rather, he is enthralled by solidarity with humanity.

Mark well: genuine love for a person is not the same as approving of his faults. Of course, by 'faults' are not meant the shortcomings and limitations which each person has in one way or another. Love for the other presupposes that we respect a person's unique nature and that we simply take his faults of character along with it. When the Rule speaks of aversion for someone's faults, serious moral faults are meant. Evil and wrongdoing in this sense are always to be combated; otherwise we too become responsible for them. But even then a distinction can still be drawn between the human being and his sins. How is this possible? As I understand it, the reason may well be this: a person is never totally absorbed in his deeds; he may therefore never be identified with his fault, because there is always the possibility of change and improvement.

> Never love a person's faults, but the person himself. For God created the human being, but the faults belong to the human being himself. Love the person created by God, not the faults which belong to him. If you love

the person, you will also free him of his faults. If you love the person, you will also correct his faults. Even though you are sometimes obliged to take harsh action, do it out of love for the good of the other (*Sermons on the First Letter of John* 7, 11).

Receiving letters and gifts in secret *(11)*

These words of the Rule do require a little explanation. Certain things that for us are completely normal and taken for granted were not so in Augustine's day. The whole emphasis in this text of the Rule lies on the words 'in secret'. In antiquity a letter had in principle a public character; it was normally destined to be read by a number of people. We see this clearly if we look, for example, at the letters of Augustine himself which have been preserved; the majority of these letters are more in the nature of short tracts on various topics than communications addressed to an individual person. For us a letter is in the first place something personal, and privacy of letters is a self-evident right. That is not to say that absolutely no secret correspondence existed in antiquity. Secret correspondence, however, was almost exclusively the domain of love-letters. This explains why the Rule forbids a brother to receive letters secretly from a woman. But the Rule does not forbid all correspondence between men and women, for we know well enough that Augustine himself had a number of women correspondents.

Letters may not be received in secret, and nor may gifts. The reason for this latter is that everything one receives is first to be made available to the community. The community then divides the goods among its different members. If, therefore, a person were to receive something in secret, he would be evading this obligation.

5 SERVICE OF ONE ANOTHER

One could summarize the contents of this chapter under the following heading: service of one another on the material level. Here the household tasks which community life necessarily entails are, as it were, divided up. Food, clothes, footwear and books all have to be looked after; there is the question of health-care (public baths) and care of the sick. This is the most concrete part of the Rule because it is directly involved with ordinary day-to-day life. It will then also be obvious that this chapter contains the greatest number of time-bound elements and that therefore many of its prescriptions can no longer be lived out in the same way. There is a world of difference between the daily life of a North African of the fifth century and that of our own time. Centuries of evolution lie between, and, in this part of the Rule, the evolution is especially noticeable.

Structure:

1 Clothing held in common
2 Concern for the interests of the community as a criterion of progress
3 Public baths and care of the sick
4 Looking after one another in all our physical needs

Clothing*(1,3,4,9,11)*
In Augustine's time people did not have their own clothes as we do. Clothes were considered part of the community's property; they were stored in the one room and distributed from there. Each person simply took what he was given – if he could do so, that is, with a good grace. Willingness to wear the clothes one received was considered the ideal; on this point too, however, the Rule allows

for exceptions. But, even if there are exceptions, all the clothes must be kept in the common storeroom. Of course such a system would not work nowadays; modern hygienic standards and our present-day social conventions demand that each person wear his or her own clothes. For us a person's clothes belong to him or her. Therefore it does not make sense to adhere to this regulation any longer.

Public baths(5,7)

When the Rule speaks of 'bath' or 'baths', the Roman thermal baths are meant. We should put out of our minds the image of the bathroom or shower-recess in which we are accustomed to wash. In antiquity bathing played an important role in health-care, and many medical manuals of the time devote extensive notice to it. But only the rich could afford the luxury of a private bath. Most people had to make use of the public baths. From the time of the Caesars, however, the public bathing-places were also very luxuriously appointed. They consisted of various pools, the first of which was filled with cold water, the second with lukewarm water and the third with hot water. These bathing-places were often equipped with a sudatorium and a room where people could massage themselves with oil and ointment. While bodily hygiene and personal cleanliness would have been the major reasons for going to the baths, bathing was also prescribed for the cure of various illnesses. The curative powers of water are still recognized and used today, though to a lesser extent than in antiquity. Finally, there was the practice of taking a daily warm bath for one's own pleasure. This was a part of cultivated life; if a person could not afford to have a daily bath, he did not belong to the upper stratum of society.

It is necessary to sketch this background briefly so that

we can understand the text of the Rule. It is not surprising that religious, who by their manner of life have consciously opted to align themselves with the poor, do not go to the baths for their own pleasure, to kill the time, or to escape the intense heat in which people (especially the slaves) have to do their daily work. In the prohibition to visit the public baths merely for one's own pleasure, therefore, we can discern an element of social protest; that is, a protest against luxury and accumulated wealth, against the idleness of the privileged. But even on this point the Rule is moderate. In contrast to the many ascetics of Augustine's day who completely rejected the use of public baths, the Rule allows for exceptions if there are good reasons for them. This is determined by whether bathing in a particular instance is seen to be useful or necessary. The good health of the brothers appears here as a compelling reason; when health is at stake, one must do all one can.

Books(10)

That good care be taken of books was a matter of the utmost importance to Augustine. His great concern for his library is made known to us by his biographer Possidius, who twice comes back to the point (*Life of Augustine* 28 and 31). Indeed, in those days books were a very precious possession, for each volume had to be written by hand and therefore represented a considerable sum of money. This accounts for the seemingly strict ruling concerning the availability of books in the library. Indirectly this regulation grants us a glimpse of the importance which Augustine attached to the intellectual formation of his monks.

The inner motivation in caring for one another(2)

Despite its many, obviously time-bound, details, this chapter assumes considerable importance because of its description of the spirit and the mentality which ought to animate particular acts of caring for one another. This care for one another, also on the material level, ought to be the first obvious expression of a much deeper reality which is directly concerned with the spirituality of community life.

It is not so difficult to extrapolate from the detailed regulations concerning daily life in Augustine's time something of significance for our present-day situation. For the passage of time does not change the fact that members of a community are still obliged to see to it that each person has food and clothing. We shirk our responsibility in this matter if we keep our earnings for ourselves or profit most from them ourselves. One's wage or the gifts one receives should still in some way or other accrue to the good of the community. There are various ways in which this can come about, but, whatever way, it should not encourage a protracted immaturity in money matters. The ideal of sharing everything in common ought not to be to the detriment of personal responsibility. We have to face the fact that the community of goods cannot now be lived out in the same way as it was in the fifth century. But the inspiration that should guide us in handing over our goods to the community remains unchanged: it must prevent us from withdrawing into our shells and living only for ourselves.

Something similar could be said with regard to articles belonging to the community. These should be treated with greater care than are things meant for our own personal use. It seems to be part of human nature, however, that we assume precisely the opposite attitude: we take greater care of our own things than of goods which belong to the community. There is a number of

other ideas in this section of the Rule which are worthy
of consideration. Among them is the assertion that envy
and dissatisfaction frequently arise in connection with
material goods; Augustine is all too well aware how easily
material things become a source of division. Further, there
is the repeated warning against being at the beck and call
of one's own wishes and desires. It needs no explanation
how greatly genuine community living is threatened by
such lack of self-control, for a person's attitude is again
focused on himself without taking others into account.

Paragraph 2 begins with the words: 'The intention
behind all this is that no one will seek his own advantage
in his work. Everything you do is to be for the service of
the community. . .' Here we find the fundamental inspiration behind the concrete regulations governing daily life.
As far as material provisions are concerned, a person ought
not in the first place to be concerned about himself, but
about the other. The whole emphasis in this chapter is on
looking after the material and physical well-being *of others*.
If a person looks after himself only, he utterly disregards
the basic law of life in community, that is, love. Augustine
supports this position with several references to Paul's
hymn in praise of love. 'Love is not self-seeking' (1 Cor.
13:5); in other words, it is not love's aim to serve only its
own interests. This is Augustine's understanding of the
text of Paul, and his interpretation is closer to the intention
of the apostle than are some modern translations. Love is
essentially a stepping out of oneself and a moving towards
the other. Moreover, 'the way of love is exalted above all
other ways' (1 Cor. 12:31); that is to say, pride of place
belongs to love because it is superior to, and shines out
above, everything else. Finally, love is enduring; 'it never
passes away' (1 Cor. 13:8). Thus our temporal care for
others is given an eternal value, for love is the enduring
element in the alleviation of human needs on earth. The
needs of human beings are transitory; either they will be

alleviated in this life or they will come to an end with death.

The central idea of this chapter is found in the sentence: 'Therefore the degree to which you are concerned for the interests of the community rather than for your own, is the criterion by which you can judge how much progress you have made.' By 'progress' is meant: progress in Christian living, in the spiritual life, in love for God, or however one wishes to refer to it. In any case there is one thing that is certain: this progress depends on our love for the person alongside us. If we want to know where we stand and who we are, then we have only one trustworthy criterion according to which we can judge ourselves, and that is our concern for the interests of the community. Community in this instance should not be understood abstractly as 'the organization' or 'the institution', but the word should be taken in the sense of 'the living persons around me'. To serve the interests of the community means in the first place, for Augustine, to serve the interests of other people. And concrete love for others is, for Augustine, the equivalent of love for God. This is an idea which is central to the Rule. In the work *On the Manual Labour of Monks* 25, 32 the same idea is worded as follows:

A monk no longer seeks his own interests, but he serves the interests of Jesus Christ. . . The leaders of the earthly city of former times have been praised and held in high esteem by their historians because they put the common interests of the whole population of their city before their own interests. It even happened that one of their victorious generals who conquered Africa would have had nothing to give his daughter for her marriage, had the senate not consented to her receiving a dowry from the goods of the community. What then must be the attitude of a citizen of the eternal city, the heavenly Jerusalem, towards his community? What a monk earns through the work of his hands he should be willing to own in common with his brothers. If he lacks anything he must be prepared to be supplied with it from community property, following the words of Paul – whose precept and example he follows – 'we must be as people who possess nothing, and yet have everything' (2 Cor. 6:10).

6 LOVE AND CONFLICT

The principal theme of this chapter is common life, with the highest possible level of understanding between the members of the community. But Augustine is sufficiently realistic to know that community life without conflicts is utopian. Wherever people live side by side, there are clashes and problems. Therefore, when the Rule speaks here of unanimity among the brethren, this is not to obscure the real differences of character and temperament, of insight and opinion, of behaviour and ways of doing things. Precisely because of these differences people can enrich one another. The ideal is not the pursuit of a colourless uniformity. In every community a place must be kept for a healthy pluriformity. And it is better to acknowledge this pluriformity, which by the nature of things will always be present, than to wish to do away with it. We could therefore equally well have given to this chapter the title: on mutual forbearance. For the text is principally concerned with the right way of acting in the case of conflicts. The fact that conflicts occur is not the matter of greatest importance, but the question of how one is to respond to them.

Structure:

1 Do not allow quarrels to grow into hatred
2 Mutual forgiveness
3 Attitude towards the young people in the monastery who have not yet reached adulthood

The splinter that becomes a beam *(1)*
Quarrels must be quickly settled. The Latin word used here in the Rule is *lites,* which means fight, argument, dispute or quarrel. In opting for the translation 'quarrel' we have in mind something more than a normal difference of opinion or an ordinary conflict-situation. Differences of opinion and conflict lead people to confront one another, and this is not always a bad thing. The quarrels envisaged by the Rule, however, are more in the nature of fights. The people involved face each other as enemies, and they struggle with all their physical and mental powers to bring about the defeat of the other. In other words, their aim is to force the other person to surrender.

Fights of this kind are to be settled as quickly as possible, for otherwise 'the splinter becomes a beam'. These words clearly echo Matthew 7:3: 'Why do you observe the splinter in your brother's eye and never notice the beam in your own?' Matthew is speaking of the small faults of others at which people take offence, while they are not even aware of the much greater faults they have themselves. They see splinters in others' eyes, but not the beam in their own. As far as the text of the Rule is concerned, however, these words of Matthew are only a spontaneous reminiscence; the significance they have in Matthew is rather different from that of the Rule.

Matthew uses the symbols of splinter and beam to indicate that it is possible to see the small faults of others but to be oblivious to serious faults of one's own. On these grounds a person considers himself better than he really is and he falls into dishonesty and hypocrisy. The Rule, on the other hand, uses these symbols more to picture the process which occurs in one and the same person: splinters become beams in oneself; in other words, small things become matters of great consequence in oneself. This refers specifically to momentary outbursts of anger; if one is not careful, they grow into hatred. And, compared with hatred, anger is but a little splinter. To become angry is not so bad, but, if the angry person does not soon put an end to it, he runs the risk that his anger will assume hard and fast forms and become something permanent. While a splinter can still be taken out, to remove a beam will prove insuperable; for a beam is so heavy that it cannot be lifted up and carried away. An image of this kind was known to Augustine from the profane literature of his time which described hatred as 'deeply rooted anger'.

In order to have a full understanding of this text of the Rule, it is necessary to take Augustine's theology of hatred into account. For him, hatred is related to death. This is twofold, because, when a person hates, he not only kills another but also himself. For Augustine, hatred is the exact opposite of love, the complete absence of love. Love means benevolence towards the other; therefore one wishes for the other life in its fullness, embracing the whole range of meaning that the word 'life' can have. Love, for Augustine, is life. Hatred, on the other hand, means malevolence towards the other, which is the same as wishing his death. Not without good reason does the Rule quote 1 John 3:15 at this point: 'Whoever hates his brother is a murderer.' But the results of hatred do not end there, for it also kills the hater himself.

Love is our life. If love is life, then hatred is death. When someone fears hating a person whom he loved, he in fact fears death; and this death is more merciless and more radical than the death of the body, for the soul itself is killed. You think only of someone who uses physical violence against you. But there is more to the matter than that. For what could such a person really do? Your Lord has already given you assurance with the words: 'Do not fear those who kill the body' (Matt. 10:28). By their brutal cruelty such people kill a body; but by harbouring hatred you kill a soul. They have killed another's body; you have killed your own soul (*Sermon on Psalm 54*, 7).

There is anger in the eye of another. In your eye, however, there is a beam. If you hate someone, how can you see what has to be removed from the other's eye? There is a beam in your own eye. How does this happen? The reason is that you neglect the splinter which lodged there. With that splinter you go to bed and you rise. You have cultivated it yourself, you have watered it with false suspicions, and you have fed it by giving credence to the words of flatterers and of people who came speaking ill of your friend. You have not been diligent enough to pull the splinter out, and you have made a beam of it. . . I say to you: you shall not hate. But you are quite unconcerned about it and you answer me: 'Hate, what is that? And what harm is there in a person hating his enemy?'. . . Whoever hates is a murderer (1 John 3:15). Now you can surely not say: 'What difference does it make to me if I am a murderer!'. . . You have, so to speak, done no more than to hate someone. But, in doing this, you have first killed yourself and then another (*Sermon* 49, 7, 7).

We may therefore conclude from these considerations of Augustine: where hatred reigns, death is enthroned.

Forgiving one another and praying the Our Father*(2)*

The evil which a person has unjustly caused in a moment of rage has to be made good, at least in so far as this is possible. The Rule speaks of 'healing', of restoring to health, and probably not without reason. The awful thing about causing harm to another is that it happens at all, for what is done can never be completely undone. To forgive is not the same as carrying on as if nothing had happened. To forgive means, rather, to see to it that the other is no longer treated as guilty in one's regard. The word used in the Rule is *relaxare* which means 'to be freed from guilt'; the other party no longer needs to feel guilty towards one.

Why have we to forgive one another our guilt? Literally, this sentence of the Rule reads: 'They are to forgive one another their guilt because of your prayers.' Our translation is: 'If you fail to do this (that is, forgive one another), your praying the Our Father becomes a lie.' The words 'your prayers' clearly refer to the Lord's Prayer; for, every time we pray the Our Father we say: 'as we forgive those who trespass against us'. But if we do not in fact forgive those who trespass against us, our praying the Our Father becomes a lie. The Our Father is for Augustine an agreement between God and ourselves.

> Let us then daily – and with a true heart – say: 'Forgive us our trespasses as we forgive those who trespass against us.' And, moreover, let us do what we say. We enter into a bond with God, an agreement, an engagement. The Lord your God says to you: if you forgive, then I forgive. If you do not forgive, then you, not I, uphold your guilt against yourself (*Sermon* 56, 9, 13).

Thus we may ask God to 'forgive us our trespasses', provided that we ourselves forgive our sisters and brothers. If we fail to fulfil this condition, then our prayer for forgiveness becomes a lie on two counts: first, because what we say is not true; and, second, because we do not keep to our agreement with God.

> Perhaps you have wronged someone and now wish to make good your understanding with him again. You long to say: 'Brother, forgive me that I have sinned against you.' But he has no wish to hear of forgiveness or to remit your debt. . . He should, however, be careful when he wants to pray. He was unwilling to forgive your fault; what then will he do when he begins to pray?. . . If your conscience troubles you, then pray 'Forgive us our trespasses'. But mark well, the prayer does not end there. You did not want to forgive your brother, and still you have to say 'as we forgive those who trespass against us'. Or would you prefer not to speak these words? If you do not say them, however, you do not receive anything either. Or if you say them just for the sake of saying them, you are lying. Do say them then, but speak the truth (*Sermon* 211, 3, 3).

Here we find a specific application of the principle which we have already met in chapter 2 of the Rule: our prayer is genuine only if there is harmony between the words on our lips and the intentions of our heart, between word and deed. Therefore Augustine asserts in *Sermon 1 on Psalm 103*, 19: 'If you wish to pray the Our Father with complete peace of mind, then do what you say.' In the Rule Augustine expresses this same thought very concisely: 'Indeed, the more you pray, the more honest your prayer ought to become.' And he goes a step further. In the case of someone who is never willing to ask forgiveness, Augustine says straight out that such a person does not belong in a religious community. He is there 'without reason' (*sine causa*); that is to say, his remaining in a religious community has become quite meaningless.

Everything that has been said here about forgiving and asking forgiveness is related to that love which is the aim

of life in community. A person who is never willing to
ask forgiveness, or to ask it from the heart, refuses to
live lovingly for the other. 'From the heart' means for
Augustine: with sincere humility and unfeigned love.
Thus a person who does not want to ask forgiveness
from the heart does not possess the humility which is an
essential element of love (cf. chapter 1). He thereby
becomes no better than dead wood in the community,
and the concept 'of one mind and one heart on the way
to God' no longer holds true.

Attitude towards the young people in the monastery who have not yet reached adulthood(3)

Elsewhere in his writings, too, Augustine insists that the
person who has the task of leadership in the community
should enjoy a certain respect so as to be able to exercise
his authority. It can happen that the kindness of someone
in a position of leadership may be so abused that he loses
all authority. For exercising authority is not a one-sided
matter; authority imposed one-sidedly from above is
better known as violence. True authority invariably
presupposes two persons who accept each other, for we
can only really speak of authority when we are faced with
someone who is willing to listen. Both authority and the
willingness to listen are needed for the building up of a
community, for a community cannot possibly exist
without discipline.

The Rule applies this especially to the 'young people'
(*minores*) in the monastery. Who are these young people?
We may not translate the word *minores* as 'subjects',
because the point at issue here is not the relationship
between a superior and his subjects. This text of the Rule
does not speak of one person, the superior, having
authority over everyone else in the monastery, but of a
number of persons in their relationships to one another.

Minores therefore must be related to age. It refers in fact to the youngest of all. Thus it might be translated as 'young people who have not yet reached adulthood'; and, seeing that, according to Roman law, a person did not attain his majority until he turned twenty-five, these young people need not have been all so young. Yet it is not to be excluded that even young children and adolescents lived in Augustine's monasteries. We consider that this conclusion may be drawn from *Letter* 209, 3 where Augustine describes how, under stressful circumstances, he put forward a young man called Antoninus to become bishop of Fussala. At the time Antoninus would have been between fifteen and thirty years of age. But Augustine says of him: 'He was brought up by us in the monastery from the time when he was still a child.' And in *Sermon* 355, 3 Augustine speaks of the children of Januarius who live in religious communities, the girl in a monastery of women and the boy in a monastery of men. Augustine, who is rather precise in his terminology when it comes to people's ages, uses here the word 'lad' which denotes a boy not older than fifteen. It may have been the case – confirmed, it seems to me, by recently discovered letters of Augustine – that children such as those of Januarius, whose parents could no longer look after them, were readily admitted into monastic communities.

Augustine was of the opinion that one's attitude towards these young people need not be the same as one's attitude towards adult sisters and brothers. He feared that exaggerated humility could be detrimental to the exercise of authority. Too submissive an attitude could have a counter-productive effect on the young people by making them haughty and stubborn. There are indeed other ways of making up for unduly harsh action against them; by exchanging a friendly word with them, for example, or by humbling oneself before God. It is debatable whether Augustine is right in this.

Love guided by the Spirit(3)

The Rule warns that excessive leniency or submissiveness is not necessarily genuine love. Literally, the last sentence of this chapter reads: 'The love among you ought not to be of the flesh, but should be spiritual.' The words 'flesh' and 'spirit' here have a special meaning. They do not have the meaning of an opposition between soul and body, but a biblical meaning, particularly as it is mediated to us by John and Paul. In the New Testament the word 'flesh' does not simply refer to the body, but it denotes the sinful situation in which human beings find themselves. The word 'spirit', on the other hand, refers to a life guided by God's Spirit. Thus the issue here is the opposition between the proclivity of our hearts to sin and evil and our liberation for the good by the Spirit of Christ.

Therefore it would be wrong for us to understand this sentence of the Rule as implying a rejection of the value of our physical natures. The words of the Rule are not intended as a protest against the body, for Augustine states frequently enough in his works that everyone is to love his body. And, because we are not purely spiritual beings, the question could be asked: what would our love be if it were not physical, if it were not enfleshed in some form or other through our physical natures? The Bible knows of no purely 'spiritualized' love, for, in order for it to become a reality, even love guided by the Spirit is in need of the body. Given this explanation of the concepts, it will be clear that what Augustine means by love according to the flesh is covetousness and self-seeking, to which he also imputes quarrelling, envy, slander, hatred and lust for power (*Commentary on the Letter to the Galatians* 45). In short, love according to the flesh is a love orientated to one's own ego as the focal point of everything; it is the same as egoism and false self-love. These are the opposites of genuine love which, guided by the Spirit of Christ, is mindful only of the good of the other. 'People must learn to love themselves by not loving themselves' (*Sermon* 96, 2, 2). In other words, authentic love for oneself consists in loving one's neighbour. Love means transcending our own ego. If we do this, then we do love 'spiritually' in the full sense of the word; that is, with a love that the Holy Spirit pours out into our hearts (Rom. 5:5).

7 LOVE IN AUTHORITY AND OBEDIENCE

If we can summarize the contents of this chapter under the title 'Love in Authority and Obedience', the reason is that, both in exercising authority and in obeying, the emphasis is principally on love. The inspiration at the heart of both activities must be one and the same; that is, ministering love. This chapter of the Rule is also one of the most characteristically Augustinian, because Augustine offers here a very personal vision of authority and obedience. Almost every thought reflects the personal spirituality of the author.

Structure:

1 Obey your superior
2 Duty of the superior: to serve in love, to guide and to be an example
3 Obedience as an act of compassionate love

Structure of Augustinian monastic communities*(1–4)*
It is immediately clear that Augustine's monastic communities had a very different structure from that obtaining in monasteries where the monks or sisters were

under the direction of an *abba* (father) or *amma* (mother).
This latter was the most common form of monasticism
in Augustine's time and he certainly knew of it. Yet he
went his own way, and thus he left his own mark on
the structure of his communities. In them the feature of
centralization around an *abba* or *amma* was not so strong;
and one does not have to look far for the reason. The
more democratic structure of Augustine's foundations is
undoubtedly related to the fact that, in his experience, the
religious life developed out of a group of friends. His
communities in Cassiciacum and Tagaste were clearly
made up of friends and relatives. This, of course, could
not be kept up, and we see a definite change come about
with the foundation at Hippo in 391. For Hippo Augustine
uses the word *monasterium* for the first time. This *monas-*
terium is an open community where there is room for
people coming from outside the circle of friends and
relatives.

Because Augustine's foundations arose out of a group
of friends, it is obvious that the person responsible for the
community is no longer called *abba* or *amma* but *praepos-*
itus, 'the one who is put forward', or, as it could also be
translated, 'brother prior' or 'sister prioress'. Despite the
fact that the person responsible is the leader, he is still one
of many. He remains a member of the group and there is
no essential difference between him and other members
of the group. He does not stand above the group, he
remains a part of it. Therefore he has a rather modest role
to play. For the group as a whole is emphasized more
than anything else; the mutual relationships among its
members are the matter of primary concern.

For example, it is immediately obvious that, neither in
the Rule nor in Augustine's other writings, is there any
mention of spiritual direction to be given by the leader of
the community. In the monasticism that pre-dated him,
however, it was precisely spiritual direction which formed

the most important duty of the *abba* or *amma*. In the direction given by the spiritual father or mother the members of the community heard the voice of the divine Spirit. The authority of the spiritual leaders lay principally in interpreting the call of the Holy Spirit for their followers. For Augustine, on the other hand, authority consists much more in the manifold service which one person can offer to others. Of course, according to the Rule, the community leader has specific tasks and duties which the other members of the community do not have in the same way. In the light of New Testament texts these responsibilities are summed up in this chapter of the Rule as: concern for the living out of the community ideal; action to be taken in the case of violations of that ideal; being an example oneself of fidelity to the ideals the community has set for itself (Titus 2:7); serving others in love; encouraging, supporting and being patient with them (1 Thess. 5:14). But none of these services required of authority is allotted exclusively to the community leader. In the Rule we hear repeatedly that each person is responsible for every other. Everyone must make it his or her care that the ideal is preserved, and everyone must intervene when there are serious abuses. It is not without good reason that correction and the healing of inner wounds play such an important role in community life. These are tasks for the group as a whole. The community leader, however, is assigned an exclusive role in the concluding phase of some processes; for example, he takes the final decisions in punishing transgressions. The task of the person responsible for the community is not without content, for he is ultimately the one who has to bear the burden of the whole group, even though the whole is still more important than the one person at its head. Thus we could say that, for Augustine, responsibility is not concentrated in one person, but is spread over the entire group.

In this way Augustine's communities acquire a more democratic outlook. This is not so strange if we consider that Augustine, also in religious community, pursued friendship as an ideal. But it is indeed surprising if we view the structure of his communities in the light of the social relations existing at the beginning of the fifth century. In the society of those days it was rare to find democracy and equality of rights. It is therefore possible to detect in the democratic mould of Augustine's Rule also a kind of protest against Roman society with its strongly juridical character and sharply demarcated power structures. Augustine does not simply accept the established order and adopt current ideas. On the contrary, the *monasterium* is proposed as a new form of society where the barriers between former slaves and those who were powerful landholders fall away. In the monastery everyone is given the possibility of living together with others on an equal footing, in brotherhood, and, if possible, in friendship. This is the 'new song' of which the Bible speaks.

Of course, Augustine's emphasis on community is also related to his theology, and not only to his theology of love, as we have already sufficiently established, but also to his vision of Christ. We know that he likes to represent Christ as the only teacher. People cannot bring about insight for each other. They can indeed help one another in the process of learning, but every one must come to insight and understanding personally. The truth is an event deep in our inmost being; the truth dawns on us, we say. Now, according to Augustine, all truth is learnt through the Truth that Christ is. Thus we all have one and the same interior teacher; that is, Christ. (Only by way of exception is the Holy Spirit represented by Augustine as the interior teacher.) Therefore, Christ or the Holy Spirit are the spiritual leaders around whom the whole community must gather; the community then listens as a group to Christ, the Spirit and the gospel.

The fact that Augustine in his Rule does not stress the point that religious hear the voice of God in a human being – although this idea does turn up elsewhere in his work – amounts to an important shift of emphasis. The emphasis is now laid on love rather than on faith. In this way not only authority but obedience too is placed in a different light. The focus is shifted from faith to love, although these two can never be radically separated from each other. Both directing and obeying are considered as acts of love. This is something quite out of the ordinary for us, especially with regard to obedience, because we have a centuries-old tradition behind us which approached obedience mainly as an act of faith.

Obey your superior *(1)*

In Augustine's version of Hebrews 13:17 we read: 'Obey your superiors and be subject to them; they are the ones who watch over your souls, knowing that they have to render an account of you.' In this way the author of the Letter to the Hebrews calls on the members of the early Christian communities to be docile towards their leaders, for the author is concerned about the continued existence of these communities. Augustine applies this text to the monastic community. It is of the greatest importance that there be cohesion in a religious community, otherwise it is threatened with ruin and is no longer a source of joy but of pain. Augustine probably also had in mind the continuation of Hebrews 13:17 where we read: 'Then they will do it with joy and not with sighs.'

'Obey your superior [the lay-superior and the priest] as a father,' says the Rule. With the words 'as a father' Augustine intends to bring out the atmosphere of trust and familiarity within which the relationship between superiors and other members of the community should take place. Of course, family ties do not exist between members of a religious community. As indicated by the word 'as', Augustine is only making a comparison with the family. Indeed, in this matter it is not sufficient to speak of an atmosphere of trust and familiarity; it must be accompanied by respect for the task of the superior: 'Otherwise you offend God in him.' One could perhaps surmise that Augustine is here thinking of an exceptional mode of God's presence in the superior. However, considered in the light of the closing sentence of the first chapter, 'and honour God in one another', which is said of all members of the community, it is improbable that the words 'you offend God in him' indicate a kind of exceptional position for the superior. God is personally, and therefore specially, present in each person. 'To offend God in someone' can therefore be applied to each member of the group in his or her own way. If each person is to be esteemed because God dwells there, then this certainly holds true with regard to the superior as well.

Superior–priest(1–2)
What was said earlier in this connection (see chapter 4) here becomes clear: the day-to-day running of the group falls to the lay-person, who has this responsibility even when there is a priest present in the community.

Not power but service(3)
That the meaning of authority among Christians is 'to be of service' is a favourite theme in the works of Augustine. To be in charge is to serve others; authority in the religious sense is the opposite of dominating others. The author of the Rule is entirely guided in this matter by well-known gospel texts such as Luke 22:25–6 and Mark 10:43–5. 'But

Jesus said to them: The kings of the peoples lord it over them and those who have power over them are given the title Benefactor. This must not happen with you. No; the most important among you must behave as the youngest, the person who gives orders as the one who serves' (Luke 22:25–6). 'Anyone who wants to become great among you must be your servant, and anyone who wants to be first among you must be slave to all. For the Son of Man did not come to be served but to serve. . .' (Mark 10:43–5). Moreover, the Rule clearly refers to Galatians 5:13: 'You have been called to freedom. Do not, however, abuse it as a pretext for self-seeking. Serve one another, rather, through love.'

It is not surprising that the passages of the Rule concerning authority and office correspond literally to what Augustine says of his function as bishop, for in both cases the same evangelical inspiration is at work. 'Even though we as bishop appear to address you from a higher place, yet we lie full of fear at your feet, since we are all too well aware of the great and hazardous responsibility our office requires of us' (*Sermon* 146, 1, 1; *Sermon on Psalm 66*, 10). 'I implore you, beloved sisters and brothers, have compassion on me, even though you have forgotten your responsibility towards yourselves' (*Sermon* 232, 8, 8). Augustine never considered office as an honour, but always as a burden (*sarcina*, that is, the baggage which a soldier had to carry on his back). Therefore, the person responsible for the group has his place not so much at the top of the community, but rather at its base. The Rule expresses this idea in a fine antithesis: because of your esteem for him, the person bearing responsibility shall be your superior; because of his responsibility to God, however, he shall be the least of all.

Because of your esteem he is your superior*(3)*

The Rule connects a person's being a superior with the esteem which others have for him. We sometimes do not pay sufficient attention to this important connection and to the substantial interaction between these two. No one can be a superior unless others esteem and value him as such. Thus a person may well be appointed leader of a group and charged with responsibility for it, but, unless there are also people who accept this leadership, nothing will come of it in everyday life. Only when a summons is answered does it really become a summons; otherwise it will remain an empty word. In this sense our esteem makes another our superior. Conversely, this means too that the members of a group can emasculate the function of leadership and make the leader's task impossible. No one is our superior by nature, but, because of our commitment, we make another person our superior; thus our free choice and co-operation are presupposed. To esteem another more highly than ourselves (Phil. 2:3) is of importance not only in our relationship to the superior; it is also a basic law in our ordinary day-to-day contact with one another.

Because of his responsibility he shall be the least of all*(3)*

While we make another person our superior, God makes him the least of all. Notice the twofold contrast: ourselves – God; superior – least of all. Because of his responsibility the superior is the least of all with regard to God. This means that his responsibility to God is greater than that of others because he has been charged with the care of all. Thus 'the least of all' here has the meaning 'he who serves most'. We have interpreted the Latin text of the Rule in this sense; literally, it reads: 'In fear before God shall the one who has responsibility for you lie under your feet.'

It will be evident that the word 'fear' in this context is related to the bearing of responsibility. When we speak of a person being responsible for others, the question automatically comes up whether, in the eyes of God, he is doing it well. The thought that an account has to be rendered to God forces the person, as it were, to examine his conscience continually; for, in his relationship to his fellow human beings, each person stands at the same time before God.

'To lie under your feet' is an ancient expression full of symbolism; it also occurs frequently in the Bible. The feet are the lowest part of the human figure. Therefore, a person who lies under another's feet is the lowest, the least of all. We are familiar with the image of the victor who places his foot on the vanquished. But this scenario of violence and force is not intended here. Augustine is referring rather to someone who freely chooses to serve others and who, by doing so, shows his desire to be less than others.

Love–respect(3)

It should be one's object more to be loved by others than to be feared: this is a thought that recurs repeatedly in Augustine. In his time this principle also constituted the ideal line of conduct for politicians. From a Christian perspective, however, there is a certain danger attached to this; it is strikingly described in *Confessions* 10, 36, 59:

> This is why the enemy of our true happiness persists in his attacks upon me, for he knows that when men hold certain offices in human society, it is necessary that they should be loved and feared by other men. He sets his traps about me, baiting them with the tributes of applause, in the hope that in my eagerness to listen I may be caught off my guard. He wants me to divorce

my joy from your truth, O Lord, and place it in man's duplicity. He wants me to enjoy being loved and feared by others, not for your sake, but in your place. . . Let us glory in you alone. If we are loved by others let it be for your sake. And let your word be feared in us.

'Fear' in this text is used in the sense of respect, not of anxiety. According to Augustine, people really ought not to be afraid of one another, because they are all equally limited and mortal (*Sermon* 65, 1, 2). Thus he consistently distinguishes between two kinds of fear and two kinds of slavery. There is a slavish fear, which is afraid of punishment. But there is also an honourable fear which is characterized by the concern that love will not be lost; this applies both to the love which I myself have and to the love which another person has for me. And, just as there are different kinds of fear, so there are different forms of slavery. There is the slave who acts only out of fear; but there is also the slave who serves out of friendship. Slavish fear and love do not go together, but honourable fear and love do. The most one can say of slavish fear is that it is a kind of preparation for love. To the extent that love grows, however, slavish fear decreases; the greater the love, the smaller the fear. Yet, according to Augustine, even in the purest of loves an element of fear is still preserved; this he will call honourable fear. It is the fear of losing a person we love or the fear of being separated from a loved one. This kind of fear springs from love itself and is an essential aspect of it. We understand now why the Rule connects love and fear with each other. For all genuine love necessarily includes reverence and respect, even if solely because of the fact that the person loved is different from ourselves. There can be no love without a fundamental reverence for the other.

When the Rule speaks of 'fear' in this connection, it is not out of the question that Augustine may also have in mind the fear of shortcomings in living up to the ideal demanded of members of the community. In this respect the text quoted from the *Confessions* is very illuminating. We read there that it is not the person of the superior who has to be feared, but the word of God which he speaks. For the superior derives his authority from that word of God. Of himself the superior has no authority or power over others. He is not a god, and he ought not to put himself in God's place. In fact he is required to render an account to God precisely for his conduct towards the other members of the community. He can never say that no one has the right to call him to account, because his function as superior neither originates in himself nor does it end there. The whole community is the listening subject who hearkens to the word of God. The superior too, as a member of the community, stands under the authority of the word of God.

Compassion with yourselves and with the superior *(4)*

The question of obedience is now raised briefly and pithily. A community is built up not only by the authority of the superior but also by the love and the willingness to listen displayed by its members. The Rule represents obedience as an act of compassion. This compassion is, however, twofold: a person is to have compassion not only on himself, but also on the superior. Of course, the Rule is not speaking of pity in the sense of a sentimental feeling, but of an act of mercy and goodness. It is a matter of opening one's heart to a poor person. We have to begin from the fact that each person is poor *vis-à-vis* God. Everyone is imperfect and still a long way from being wholly good. But we are capable of doing something to overcome our inner poverty. For we can love what is good. And anyone who loves what is good combats his

own limitations and contributes in the best possible way
to his own self-unfolding.

The sentence from the Rule reads: 'By your ready and
loving obedience, therefore, you not only show compassion to yourselves, but also to your superior.' In order to
understand fully the thinking behind this, we have to go
back to the text of Jesus Sirach by which Augustine was
inspired. In modern translation Sirach 30:23 reads: 'Seek
distraction from your cares, console your heart, chase
sorrow far away; for sorrow has been the ruin of many.'
Augustine, however, had before him an entirely different
reading of Sirach 30:23: 'And show compassion to your
own soul by pleasing God.' Augustine commented on this
text on a number of occasions. His explanation of it could
be succinctly outlined as follows: life teaches us that we
find ourselves in a situation of spiritual poverty; only God
can alleviate this situation; therefore for us to love God is
the greatest service we can do ourselves (*The City of God*
21, 27, 2). To live uprightly and in goodness from the
love which God has given us: this is the first act of charity
which we can and must perform for ourselves. Whoever
lives in wickedness hates himself; for he is not merciful
but cruel to himself (*Enchiridion on Faith, Hope and Love*
20, 76). Thus a person has to have compassion on himself,
in so far as he has always to care for his own well-being.
And this well-being comprises more than just material
sufficiency, for, with that alone, one would still fall short
of the ultimate goal in life. Thus a person cares for his
own well-being in the full sense of the word, only if he
is in the first place interested in looking after his spiritual
well-being. Anyone who neglects that in fact hates
himself; he brings death upon himself. In the light of this
explanation it will be clear that compassion in this context
has nothing to do with self-pity or with ego–centredness.
What is at stake is genuine concern for the deepest
meaning of life, and this is to be found in love for God

and for one another. To obey the superior or to listen to
one another (for obedience is not limited to listening to
the superior alone) is for Augustine primarily an act of
love. In practising love we contribute to our own salvation
and we show that our hearts are open to ourselves as
creatures who are on the way to God.

At the same time, however, obedience is also an act of
mercy to the superior. We already know that Augustine
considers the office of superior not as an honour or a
dignity, but as a burden. In this way obedience can be
understood as lightening the oppressive burden of
another. The other members of the community allow the
burden borne by the one responsible for the group to
weigh on them as well; they too bear this burden; together
they put their shoulders to the task. This appears very
clearly in the words addressed by Augustine, in one of his
works, to a group of monks:

> If, after our reprimand – or, rather, after our urgent
> request – you are still of a mind to persevere in your
> recalcitrant attitude, then I can do no more than to be
> sad and to mourn. But you must know how things
> stand. That is enough. If you are servants of God, you
> will have mercy on me. But if you do not show me
> compassion, I still do not wish to use stronger language
> (*On the Manual Labour of Monks* 33, 41).

In the final sentence of this chapter Augustine indicates in
yet another way that obedience is an act of love. He
emphasizes that authority is a dangerous burden: '. . . the
higher the position a person holds, the greater the danger
he is in.' The duty of leadership and the threat of danger
go hand in hand for Augustine. The reason for this is that
all people in official positions are liable to be tempted to
consolidate their own power rather than to use their position as a service for the good of others. Augustine calls
this the temptation to domination, the temptation result-

ing from the dangers present in giving leadership to others (*Sermon on Psalm 106*, 7). We can therefore conclude: all that has been said on authority and obedience has shown the strong propensity of Augustine to deal with these questions in the context of mutual love.

8 CONCLUDING EXHORTATION

This final chapter of the Rule is more than just a conclusion. It directs us to the foundations of religious community and to the goal pursued there. The concluding exhortation opens with the words: 'May the Lord grant that, filled with longing for spiritual beauty, you will lovingly observe all that has been written here.' This is strongly reminiscent of the first sentence of the Rule: 'We urge you who form a religious community to put the following precepts into practice . . . on the way to God.' In the previous chapters Augustine has given practical norms to be applied in everyday life. Now he dwells for a moment on the spirit with which these rules of life are to be observed.

Structure:

1   Desire for spiritual beauty
2   The life-giving aroma of Christ
3   Free under grace
4   As in a mirror

Desire for spiritual beauty*(1)*
The spirit with which the precepts given ought to be carried out is described as love for spiritual beauty. The

loving desire for spiritual beauty is to be the foundation of our action. But spiritual beauty is also the goal which we are approaching. What Augustine means by spiritual beauty is the highest, the divine beauty (*On Eighty-three Different Questions* 30). Furthermore, in Augustine, the concept of beauty is always linked to another idea, namely, that of contemplative enjoyment. Compared to the beauty of the world which we encounter on our pilgrim journey through this life, divine beauty shines forth as the ultimate beauty. We hope to enjoy this beauty eternally, and it will bring us the soundest rest and deepest peace. In this way love for God is presented as the source and final goal not only of the Christian life as such, but also of the religious life.

Augustine frequently passes over from the divine beauty to Christ, who 'surpasses everyone in beauty' (Ps. 45:3), but who, for the sake of others, 'became a man of sorrows, without looks or beauty to attract our eyes' (Isa. 53:2–3). (Cf. *On Holy Virginity* 54, 55.) In this way, Augustine as it were, calls us back from the eschatological dream to the reality of this life. He does the same thing here in the Rule. Having mentioned the divine beauty, he immediately passes over to Christ. In the present time, for us to love divine beauty is nothing other than to radiate the example of Christ through the conduct of our lives.

And thus we come to the meaning of spiritual beauty as that beauty which we are to realize in our way of living through the practice of love. Augustine expresses this splendidly in his *Sermons on the First Letter of John* (9, 9): 'We shall come to possess beauty by loving him who always remains beautiful. According as love grows in you, beauty grows too. For love is the beauty of the soul.'

To spread the life-giving aroma of Christ*(1)*
This image of a fragrance which spreads further and further is taken from 2 Corinthians 2:15. It reminds us in the first instance of the incensings which were offered to God in the temple. Just as incense has a pleasant aroma, so too must our life be pleasant before God. But this image also has a missionary dimension; it points to our mission as Christians. It is through us that the figure of Christ has to be formed in this world. The importance and the value of following Christ are made clear to others not so much by words as by the kind of lives we lead. Our personal conduct and our own concrete choices are the best proclamation of Christ. 'If there is anyone among you who wishes to be known for his wisdom and learning, he must prove such a claim by the excellence of his life' (James 3:13). This holds for religious as well: their lives must show forth Christ's power of attraction.

Not as slaves – but as those who are free*(1)*
These words are an allusion to Romans 6:14–18: 'Sin should not dominate you, since you are living by grace and not by the law. . . You are, thank God, no longer slaves of sin. . . You have been freed from the mastery of sin. . .' Another Pauline text also springs to mind in this regard: 'Where the Spirit of the Lord is, there is freedom' (2 Cor. 3:17). Augustine, by combining these two Pauline texts, has come up with the contrast: slaves under the law – free men under grace. For those who believe in him Christ means freedom, but not freedom in the sense of being completely without ties. A Christian does not live without any law at all. The point at issue in Pauline theology is the liberation through Christ from the dominating power of sin. Augustine is very much under the influence of Paul on this point. For Augustine, the most important characteristics of our liberation through Christ

are love ('Love is the fulfilment of the Law': Rom. 13:10) and bearing one another's burdens ('Bear one another's burdens, and thus you will fulfil the Law of Christ': Gal. 6:2).

In Augustine's vision, love and freedom belong together. In his own words: 'We are no longer under the Law which, while it commands the good, is unable to give it. On the contrary, we are under grace which, in making us love what the Law commands, can reign over us as free people' (*On Continence* 3, 8).

Why at this point in his Rule does Augustine introduce this composite brief reference to the theology of grace? The reason may well be that it links up directly with the sentence preceding it, which dealt with following Christ in our own lives. The spirit in which this is to be done is now made clear: not as slaves, but as free men and women. We are not slaves, who perform what is required of them only out of fear. Through grace we enjoy a childlike freedom which enables us to face God full of confidence. Our freedom does not mean that we no longer recognize precepts or laws; it means, rather, that we can rely on the grace of Christ who gives us the power to fulfil the law of Christ, which is love, and which includes all other precepts.

So much for the general theological background to the words: 'not as slaves – but as free men and women'. It was also Augustine's wish to apply the contrast slave – free to his Rule. His Rule is not intended as a detailed system of laws which crush the human person and make a slave of him, but as a call to a life in joy and freedom made possible by the abundance of Christ's grace. Throughout the Rule this freedom under grace finds expression; for it can be seen at a glance how few concrete prescriptions or detailed defined norms are given in the Rule. No order of the day is to be found, nor is there any hard and fast way of organizing community living; the

Rule consists instead of several fundamental principles to which we should look for inspiration. Augustine was never the man for a host of precepts and laws; rather, he was a person always in search of the essential, in pursuit of the inner core of things and of the human heart. On his very first acquaintance with monastic life Augustine was struck by its freedom, and it is surely no accident that he gave the following description of the religious life as he first came to know it in Milan and Rome: 'They live together there in Christian love, in holiness and in freedom' (*The Way of Life of the Catholic Church* 1, 33, 70). Freedom appears as a characteristic of the religious life, along with love and holiness. Freedom must, therefore, have been an important element of the religious life for Augustine.

As in a mirror(2)

The classical image of the mirror in which a person looks at himself is also found in James 1:23–5: 'Whoever listens to the word but does not obey it is like a man who looks at his own features in a mirror, and then, after a quick look, goes off and immediately forgets what he looked like. But whoever considers himself in the light of the perfect law of freedom, and makes that his habit – not listening and then forgetting, but actively putting it into practice – will be blessed for what he does.' Christians must mirror themselves on the word of the Lord in order to see if they are living according to the ideal held up to them. This will be the case only if the believing acceptance of Jesus' message shows itself in action in everyday life. For God's will is proclaimed with a view to its being done. Looking in the mirror must result in some practical influence on life; this influence will be expressed mainly in loving one's neighbour. Otherwise our faith is but self-deception.

Augustine uses this image of the mirror very frequently. Usually he applies it to the Scriptures, but he also uses it in relation to the apostolic confession of faith, the commandments of God, and even in relation to his own teaching. This last-mentioned application is not so surprising, for the instruction which Augustine gives has no other purpose than to show forth or to mirror the Scriptures. In the same sense he also calls his Rule a mirror. Because of the evangelical inspiration which the Rule offers, it too is an exhortation to live and act in the spirit of Christ. What is said in the Rule is like a mirror in which we are to look regularly in order to see whether we are neglecting or forgetting anything. Practice has taught us, however, that having the Rule read aloud each week rapidly degenerates into an uninspiring routine. Anything repeated too often soon begins to sound hackneyed; the meaning and the power go out of it. Therefore, it would perhaps be better to read it in parts; these could, for example, be inserted into community prayer or into some other community exercise.

Living up to the ideal – failure*(2)*
The final sentence of the Rule reveals a threefold structure: present–past–future. Augustine frequently uses such a structure at the conclusion of his expositions. Here he develops it:

1   If you now find that your actions match what you read in this mirror, then give thanks to the Lord.
2   But if you see that you have failed in the past, then pray that God will forgive your guilt.
3   And, as for the future, ask God that you will not be put to the test.

As we may have expected from the doctor of grace, the Rule ends with a song of praise to the Lord, the giver of

all good. For all the good in us is not our own achieve-
ment, but ultimately God's gift. This idea is entirely in
harmony with Augustine's well-known assertion: 'Even
our merits are God's gifts' (*Sermon* 298, 5, 5). Thus the
good in us cannot but be a source of gratitude.

The fact that we have failed, however, ought not to be
a reason for despair. The Lord's Prayer contains God's
promise that our sins will be forgiven, if we really forgive
our sisters and brothers. It was Augustine's constant
conviction that even our transgressions can play a positive
role. Indeed, his own life provides a vivid example of this.
The great emphasis he gave to grace never made him a
pessimist. Therefore Augustine can see even in a person's
sins the possibility of bringing about some good for him.
And the good is to be found in the humility a person
learns and in a proper appreciation of his own standing
before God. Faults – if they are dealt with for the good –
are an antidote to pride, which imprisons a person in
himself. 'For those who love God, he works all things for
good. And this "all" takes in so much that, even if a
person deviates from and leaves the right path, he is
enabled to make progress in good, for he returns more
humble and more experienced' (*On Rebuke and Grace* 9,
24).

Only the childlike person is open; he waits for another,
he waits for the Other. To limit ourselves to the former,
that is, to our openness for one another, it will be clear
that we can understand each other much better if we are
conscious of our own shortcomings. Then we will be
much less closed to others and less inclined to lecture them
or to reject them. Thus even our failures can provide the
occasion for loving more deeply, and love is the goal of
all things. We ask in prayer that we may not fall prey to
the temptation to distorted self-love, but that genuine love
may ever be preserved in our midst so that we can always
sincerely pray the 'Our' Father.

5H

Printed in the United States
by Baker & Taylor Publisher Services